The Jeweled Net of Indra

poems by

Dane Cervine

Plain View Press
P. O. 42255
Austin, TX 78704

plainviewpress.net
sbright1@austin.rr.com
1-512-440-7139

The metaphor of Indra's Net is attributed to an ancient Buddhist teacher named Tu-Shun (557-640 B.C.E.), who envisioned life as a vast net with a jewel at each juncture. Each jewel, representing an individual life form, atom, cell or unit of consciousness, reflects all the other jewels in a cosmic matrix and is intrinsically and intimately connected to all others. A change in one gem is reflected in all the others.

The image of Indra's Net conveys that the compassionate and constructive contribution a person makes produces a ripple effect of beneficial action that reverberates throughout the universe. By the same token, one strand of the net cannot be damaged without damaging the others or setting off a cascading effect of destruction

.

Acknowledgements

The Jeweled Net of Indra: **The SUN Magazine**, as well as **Poetry Flash**; Adrienne Rich chose this poem as the winning entry in the National Writers Union 2005 contest, along with *Holography* for Honorable Mention. *Holography, Dark Flowers Speaking,* and *The Last Days:* **Monterey Poetry Review.** *Engine:* **The SUN Magazine.** *Where The Grass Is Greener:* **Porter Gulch Review,** where Dane was chosen as the 2006 **Poet of the Year Winner.** *A Crack Between Two Worlds; Grateful Deadheads Talk Trash At The Café; Blue In The Face, Oh Say Can You See,* also appeared in the **Porter Gulch Review.** *Absent War's Preoccupations* and *Outside The Cathedral:* **POEM.** *Fundamentals* and *Poetry Should:* **Buckle &.** *A Pearl of Great Price:* **Rockhurst Review.** *Every Story Is Mine:* **Studio One,** as well as **Out of Line: Imaginative Writings On Peace and Social Justice.** *The Small Body of the Human:* **Amoskeag: Journal of Southern New Hampshire University.** *Norte Americano:* **Raven Chronicles 9/11 Edition: Neutral Air.** *How The World Changes:* **Raven Chronicles.** *Omens:* **Branches Quarterly.** *Leaning Towards The Southern Hemisphere:* **POETALK.** *My Daughter Reads The Morning Paper:* **Out of Line: Imaginative Writings On Peace and Social Justice.** *This Burning:* **Sacred Fire Anthology** by Adams Media. *Peace March:* **Tapestries Anthology,** as well as the **Poetry Santa Cruz Chapbook 2002.** *Radar:* **The Awakenings Review.** *Lions In Slumber:* the anthology **Working For The Money: Poems of the Working Poor** by Bottom Dog Press, along with *Radar. I Am A White Man:* **U.S. Latino Review,** with another version appearing in the **Porter Gulch Review.** *After The Earthquake:* **Permafrost,** as well as the **Santa Cruz SENTINEL Spotlight.** *Secret Dreams of Committees:* **ZamBomba.** *Dante's Spoons:* **Rock and Sling.**

Many of the poems in this book also appeared in earlier chapbooks published by the author as **One Pony Press** editions.

Contents

Every Story Is Mine   11

The Jeweled Net of Indra   13
Every Story Is Mine   14
The Last Days   15
Holography   17
After the Earthquake   18
Savoring the World   19
Speed, Grit, Radiance   21
My Daughter Reads the Morning Paper   22
May the Serpent Be Unbroken   23
Surfaces   24
Prayers In a Vortex   25

Oh Say Can You See   27

Oh Say Can You See   29
At the Russian River   31
Half Full, Half Empty   32
Allah's Garden   32
Where the Grass Is Greener Still   33
A Rose, a Thorn   34
A Pearl Of Great Price   35
What Does It Mean To Be Safe At Home?   36
Hubris   37
Engine   38
Destinations Unknown   39
Breakfast On the Haight   40
Altered States Of America   41
Radar   42
Sweet Trivia   44
Of Wood and Steel   45
Emergency Procedures   46
What We Have To Offer   48
What We Cannot See   49
Behemoth   50

This American Life   52
I Am a White Man   53
Spectrum   55
Norte Americano   56
Omens   57
Leaning Towards The Southern Hemisphere   58
Full Moon In Costa Rica   59
One World   61
Grateful Deadheads Talk Trash At the Café   62
Failure To Notice the Signs   63
Alternative Evangelism   64
Patriotism   65

Dark Flowers Speaking   67

Dark Flowers Speaking   69
Why Men In Wartime Are Not To Be Trusted   70
Who Could Dream Such Horrible Beauty?   70
The War To End All Wars   71
The Battle For Our Hearts   72
War   73
Motivation   73
Everyman   74
No Surrender   74
Something In Us   75
A Prayer For Less   75
Rainy Morning   76
Enough   76
The Weather In Our Hearts   77
Another Christmas Story   77
Absent War's Preoccupations   78
Small Dreams   79
Of Shoes & Missiles   81
Peace March   82
Silhouettes   83
All Hallows Eve   85
Napa Valley, Before the End   86
Ozone's Koan   87

Fundamentals   88
Higher Than Birds   89
Manifest Destiny   90
The Weather Gods   90
This Remembering   91
Heaven On Earth   92
What We Might Become   93

A Crack Between Two Worlds   95

A Crack Between Two Worlds   97
The Middle World Where We Live   98
The Spell   99
The Cage   100
Prophecy   102
What Is It Worth   102
The Small Body Of the Human   103
Blue In the Face   104
Sizing Up the World   106
Universal Studios   107
Nebuchadnezzar's Stone   108
At San Marcos Square   108
Outside the Cathedral   109
Surrender   109
Fear, Skin, Power   110
The Lost Goddess   110
Food For Thought   111
Abandoned Clay   111
Island Of the Sharers   112
The Endless Quest   112
Witnessing   113
Another Ordinary Day   113
A Cure For What Is Human   114
Am I Awake Or Asleep?   114
Dante's Spoons   115
The Secret Dreams Of Committees   117
HEARTHEARTHEARTHEARTH . . .   119
The Shining Path   120

Atop the Parking Garage In Downtown Sacramento   121
This Burning   122
Emancipation   124
Writers In the Schools   124
Leaving a Mark   125
When Justice Goes Blind   125
Lions After Slumber   126
How the World Changes   128
Poetry Should   130

Notes   133
About the Author   135

*You have to tell the truth in poetry. You have to
be willing to say what you think, and be wrong, and
fall on your face, and have jaded sophisticates laugh
at your naiveté, and have cool populists laugh at
your pompous elitism...You have to respect the deep
seriousness of the act of writing a poem and be willing
to stand behind what you have written....*

Campbell McGrath, in *Fugue*

Every Story Is Mine

The Jeweled Net of Indra

Driving down the freeway, remembering Hindu mythology—Indra's net, each intersecting weave holding a jewel reflecting every other facet of every other jewel, infinitely. Suddenly, I see the hands that paint the white lines, that lay the black asphalt, hands of a man joyous or lost soap-scrubbing his body clean for dinner and beer, for the wife who loves him, hands that hold their tickets for London to see the grandmother, the hard-drinking pub matron whose body bore children in building rubble when the Nazi bombing relented—and if not for that war, would I be driving now, hands on the wheel, listening to the radio recount the birth of the child named Tsunami after the storm that drove her mother into the hills, would the meager dollars I send to rebuild a village—minted with the Rosicrucian-eye above the pyramid dreamed by this country's founders as the all-seeing vision of a world where not a sparrow falls that we don't know about—would I have known to send it, if not for the hands that flew the kite that drew electricity from the skies that made its way into the flat-screened box that unveils this jewel-linked world twenty-four hours of every gleaming day, weaving news with advertisements for clothes made by hands in China nimbly sewing a dream of Hollywood and Ipod and offering their bodies one by one for a better future—while the coal that fumes the electricity that plunges the needle drifts in air that circles a globe that warms the icecaps that melt into sea that shifts the current that loves the wind that swirls from heaven to earth stirring one storm after another, blowing its diaphanous passion over New Orleans like a trumpet sinking the heart so low with blue notes that flood is a dark cure for what burns—this illusion that anyone stands alone—stranded on the roofs of our swollen houses mouthing save me to a world whose millions of hands can turn up the volume loud enough to finally hear, or flick with a single click the entire interconnected vision of it all off.

Every Story Is Mine

Fearless, I open the newspaper another day,
unroll the modern parchment, this divine scroll,
unfathomable. A quick scan of the headlines,
the fine print of each obituary.

There is never enough tragedy
to ensure your own safety.

Dressing for work, I pray the day's gauntlet
escapes the evening news, that I return home
unscathed, intact.

Fate is impenetrable. This is why every horoscope,
tea leaf, chicken bone clattering to the ground as dice
holds such fascination—will we become
what we fear, what we hope?

Every step away brings me closer to what I run from.

If I were to let the world roll through me as a flood,
would I be saved, or merely drown?

There are no answers to such questions,
though the front page begs each one.

I finger each tattered edge, laughing, crying.
Every story is mine.

The Last Days

My daughter looks up from the Sunday news—
an earthquake in Pakistan, the many dead—
betrays a quick glance of fear, after so many
hurricanes these last days, New Orleans flooded,
Texas evacuated, Florida bracing, Indonesia
reeling from the last tsunami. The book
of Revelations lies in my childhood memory,
prophecy of flood, famine, fear—but I
can't bear to tell her my secret misgivings,
that I am nearly fifty, peering down the gauntlet
of my own last days, wondering how to spend
judiciously, extravagantly, each one of them.
But this is all so personal, a sin, really,
when living in the belly of an empire
bent on catapulting us into the next war,
the next bald-faced robbery of a planet's future
for this year's money-grab, the whole world
aghast and envious of this drunken bully
staggering belligerently towards oil
like an addict who would do
          anything, anything
for just one more fix. But I am no prophet,
succumb to the small world of breakfast
my daughter and I share, intimate,
in these last days of childhood, poised
as she is on the lip of a world that would
just as soon devour as kiss her, and
how can I prepare her for this rogue?
The way fear's scripture insinuates its way
into the petty concerns of a life lashed
to the mundane but longing for revelation,
for some final reckoning. How do I say

I love you when this world is the only gift,
the pitiless dowry, I have to offer? How
do I say *it is you*, your brother, your friends,
the only hope for this brooding planet,
a new seed of reluctant messiahs peering
at the earth you shall inherit from us—
this thin, ephemeral line between
Eden and Armageddon.

Holography

Coal country, West Virginia—I walk into a diner,
past the $100,000 reward poster in the window
for the sniper who shot Jeannie at the Speedway.
Our waitress—a poised old dame—
carries herself, effortlessly and without pride,
as the hidden center of a universe, and maybe
like Jeannie, she is, for someone. I open my book,
The Passion of Western Philosophy, wait for eggs,
bacon, biscuits, read about the Copernican revolution—
the earth no longer the center of things,
a peripheral sphere lost on the edge of an endless
black cosmos amid small blazing lights. Maybe
this is what Jeannie's lover felt—the empty year
reeling out of orbit, no gravity, lost
in a centerless universe blown wide.
Then, like Nietzsche, killing his own god
in the bleak landscape of a world edged
on the abyss. But looking into the waitress' eyes
as she says *thanks hon* for the extra tip,
I feel this universe circling back inside me—
Jeannie, her stalking lover, the beating
of a billion galaxies sounding here,
the *thump-thump* inside this chest,
the aching muscle at the heart of it all.

After the Earthquake

I became fascinated with old benches,
old theater pews
saved from demolition

like the ones from Café Pergolesi
behind the old bookshop
before the big quake.

I'd wander from cafe to cafe
sitting in each wooden chair found,
dispersed in second hand sales
across town,

the soft weathered touch
a sign-post of survival

that one can be found
again and again

even after the earth
opens
to take you from
all you know.

Savoring the World

Washington DC, a warm evening in November,
sitting outside the Sultan's Palace waiting for a gyro,
sipping Almaza beer while the world rolls by,
students from Georgetown & Howard universities
chattering on cell phones, and I have never been so happy
to be alone, listening, open as a gate in this corner chair,
the sensory soup of neighborhood, globe,
anywhere I look *seeing* what God was aiming at,
the words *ordinary, mundane* made up later
by those with a short attention span. *Look!*
at the silver sport utility vehicle gliding by,
windows rolled down, blaring bass syncopating
with the sirens searing down the adjacent block:
could it get any better than *this!* And the faces
of Arab, African, & Asian so at ease you could almost believe
the Shoe Repair sign across the street:
that anything broken can be mended, here

.

And so I listen to the bald man in white shirt,
white slacks, white shoes tell his cell phone
my brother died of AIDS ten years ago, and I'm still grieving.
And how the jaunty-capped black man lights up
with *Mother!* as his cell phone jingles, flips open,
carries the voice of the one he loves. Listen
to how the world can only be what it is—
invoke the sirens circling now like dogs
to keep at bay the rabid snarl of wanting things
to be other than they are. Like the blond woman
in the crosswalk just now, two Dobermans leashed
& serene: there's no fathoming what goes on inside,
the political science of hormone & heart begging détente,
a kind of soul you could actually live in.

So when my gyro comes—all tactile & aroma—
every taste bud kneels down, prays
that this pepper mixed with sweet bean,
this flesh of fowl & wheat, be its own sacrament—
savoring the carnal world sacred.

Speed, Grit, Radiance

Flying over the frozen brown of Nevada, shades of tanned lace, khaki, animal hide. In the plane, not many passengers. I stretch out, doze in the illusion of stillness, till white cloud through window is pierced by a small dart of black, like a distant crow: another plane moving at such speed the other way—I see how fast, how fragile.

Then over Chicago, a great train yard, row upon row of rusted burgundy box-cars, then multi-hued, forming a gritty rainbow in the tough urban sprawl of track and abandoned brick. What it takes to live on the ground: a body that can bear grief like iron rails, like old timber.

In Washington DC, the Ethiopian cab-driver is happy with my questions, tells me of his fifteen years here, four in Missouri before. But Yugoslavia was the friendliest, he says, where he felt the most at home—before the ethnic cleansing, the death. And I notice, outside the window: orange leaves blowing past the orange hood, how beautiful the falling, the way they are carried, the radiance.

My Daughter Reads the Morning Paper

She opens the world
as a present unwrapped slowly,
unsure if it might be her heart's desire,
or a sensible pair of socks to replace the one
with holes. Unraveling the morning paper,
she comes to expect the small wars,
the persistent headlines about this tragedy
or that, the occasional stories of everyday people
triumphing against the odds. Mostly she loves
the comics, the heroism of sports, learning
the world's humor, a taste for winning.
Twelve years of tenderness are woven
through the strands of her heart,
the softly spun gray matter
cupped in her skull more precious
than radium or plutonium, the potent
half-life of her soul glowing now
as it meets the lost half of the world:
I hear it calling her in the earthquakes of Iran,
the tin-cities of Brazil, the picture on the back page,
the one she doesn't mention, the one
she peers at as though the world, unwrapped,
was more than she could dare
to care this much for.

May the Serpent Be Unbroken

Deep in Costa Rica, by a stream in lush jungle
lives a woman who paints. She leads us into a room,
pulls an immense leather satchel from the closet, opens it—
sheaths of canvas thick with colored oils,
mostly of the black women of Limon,
large hands & bodies expressive because she could not speak
the language, could not say what she saw, could only show.
I ask how she arrived here:

white Quaker woman with bearded husband
who makes affordable bamboo housing that will one day
save the world—and the acres next door,
planted with a hundred varieties of bamboo:
the one, thick as your arm, that grows six inches
a day—you can sit, watch the world grow.
She says you just climb into a beaten VW van
before you know

where you are going, drive through Mexico,
Guatemala, Nicaragua before you know to worry,
land along a coast where old conquistador blood
mixes with indigenous, mixes again with black Caribbean—
and in the face of a world that doesn't know your name,
your language, your worth, you paint a life, a way of saving
yourself. Like the painting I buy,

composed while listening to a Cuban blues guitarist singing
May The *Serpent* Be Unbroken, rather than the *Circle*—
how the bright yellow snake appeared on her canvas,
archaic image of the old becoming new,
wrapping round the clapping woman from Limon,
biting its own tail in a perfect oval: like this painting
of an old folk tune sung wrong, every mistake
a gift, a way of making the world.

Surfaces

The smooth surface of the television screen is a terrible boundary, sterile contour lacking smell, texture—the leaking wound of distraught civilian caught in the glare of war, ooze of life spilling two-dimensional between hemorrhoid commercial and golden arch jingle. Beneath this surface lie tubes & wire, or now, plasma—further in still the digital code bounced from satellite through cable—behind even this, another code, the DNA of existence, the eye of God unblinking as a voyeur peeping through the holes in us, insatiable. All I see

in the headline's raven ink is stark contrast between the good of *us*, the evil of *them*, half truth more lie than not—a grinning confidence of fundamentalist vigor: finger of senator, editor, preacher pointing *over there*, and my own: quivering back, not believing. The surface of the moon has been touched, but it is a long way from here, where shades of skin still determine winners, losers. Beneath the smooth undulation of sea lie many secrets: fish generating their own light, lost ships, caverns plunging miles under the surface, and at the bottom, the original face each of us wears in the deep silences. It is cruel,

this failure to grasp the whole, the wide sphere of it, the way that beneath it all we are more the same than not—this thin skin of fear stretched so taut over bone that at any moment what is true in us may break out, shine.

Prayers In a Vortex

On the way to Tahoe, traffic snarls all the way through from the coast. I nap in the back seat, untangle from dreams of war, the ceaseless craving for more. Five men, old friends all, throttle down, relax. The weekend lies ahead, cheap rooms next to the ski lifts at Heavenly, the line of cars thinning as we wind through forest under darkening sky, stop for food at In' N Out Burger, wolf down hefty slabs of glistening onion, tomato, grilled meat. Another hunger follows close behind, as life consumes us, savors the taste, drizzle caught with tender tongue. Of course, we don't speak of this directly—

talk instead of work, its toll, its joys, the elusive comfort of wives, how beautiful they shine in our chests, the way we almost break each other, lives hovering somewhere between brain and bone—small triumphs floating as a grail in the shimmer of headlight along the road ahead. We arrive

in the evening, Lake Tahoe so dark as to be unseen—snow also a dim grey sheen muted in mountain shadow. Then, stepping into the perpetual day of Harrah's, we follow lined carpets through the casino towards our rooms, the omnipresent sound of tinkling slot-chimes a kind of *Om*, stubbornly happy. Here,

women shine their bodies till they glow, tuck their breasts into black velvet cups or plunging necklines of pink satin, legs layered in fishnet as though caught by the unerring cast of a thousand hopeful dreams. The men long

for a goddess emptying gold from puckered bust, the sheen assuaging the pain of abandoned houses standing vacant in the chest, porch screen banging against broken door jam, hollowness fluttering as moth wings. Television screens perch high in the bars, by the pool—constant stream of sports, live coverage of war twenty-four hours a day, simultaneous. White explosions over Baghdad, streaming tape of scores—baseball, hockey—floating beneath. I stare, unable to comprehend: *What is it we want? Why am I here?* Each garish room, each table inviting salvation, the jackpot, the right combination of numbers waiting in hand—red heart or diamond, black spade or club—your life on the line, itself a war—somber 11, passionate 7—the small yellow lemons & golden bells twirling in their cylinders, the handle pulled, fate grinning. For a moment, I think there is no escape. But outside,

snow-capped peaks form a temple, green-robed trees scattered about as hooded druids, Harrah's and Harvey's standing as huge wicker-men, a torch lit inside each so bright you'd almost expect combustion—this craving, a flame lit, the trees nodding their prayers in a vortex of wind. And the mountains, unmoved, bearing witness.

Oh Say Can You See

Oh Say Can You See

Lightning bugs glint as buoys on a dark sea, currents of air
roiling as waves from an approaching storm this fourth of July,
where Ohio and Kentucky meet, where cousins greet;
children shoot each other with water, pistols leaking
from the kitchen sink all the way outside. It is calm,
the smoldering light from Johnny's cigarette dancing
a tango in summer, tattoos gleaming as brands.
Lost cousin, he is a kind of steer, wild approaching tame,
one missing finger a medal of sorts from the Asian war,
the reason he still loves guns, his ten thousand bucks worth of bullets—
but it is the firecrackers that crack his smile now, parachutes,
black jack crackers. He stands too close to everything, everybody,
the slap-happy wide eyed stare of those who have seen too much,
can never see less again, are sure some jackpot lies deep in you
because there is nothing much left inside of them, good anyway.

Then you wonder, examining the bright yellow paint
on his 67 Chevy truck, the black Harley-Davidson leather interior
immaculately detailed, a single yellow metal chair chained to the back
behind the cab—*at least he keeps some things clean.*
You visit his house—not the bachelor bungalow you expect;
it is immaculate, gun racks ordered and dusted, but it is the flowers
in the back, an acre of flowers, that stump you—
the best thing to battle all the bad he says,
especially the black roses, fine and rare.

But you remember at dinner all the reasons to fear,
especially his fear, the rioting blacks in Cincinnati
after another young man is gunned down, but Johnny
works downtown, saw the white woman pulled from the car,
beaten, says *get back you mutha-fucka before I show you what's up,*
and in his eyes I see Viet Cong dancing behind bamboo,
behind them a father strict as a bomb, behind him a president

who gave the order, and further still those who really are
responsible, it was all of us

felt uncomfortable around Johnny, but no one would say much,
he was family, held down a job, big heart, would do anything
for you, would do anything

and then the storm came, lightning cleansing the sky
of lesser light, thunder following as great pool hall balls
cracking, breaking again and again, the moon hanging
in the sky like the last glint of Johnny's cigarette.

At the Russian River

It is the 4th of July—loud revelers stand
in the river with beers in hand, bellies big
as good-luck buddhas gone bad, noise radiating
across the gorge like imperial Americans immoveable
in the rockets red glare. All the best songs
from the seventies blare into air that tingles
with this human bombastic carnival. For a moment,

I am seduced, want to join them at drunken horseshoes,
raucous banter, because *this is our planet, our country,*
and you god-damn got it right that it's a grand party…
Watch instead from my balcony as the revelry fades—
and the big beer-belly man, who has floated down river
with his beer-bellied wife, slowly pulls her back
against the current with a rope, splayed unconscious
on her black inner-tube like the sleeping queen
of a lost country.

Half Full, Half Empty

A beaten Winnebago emblazoned with *Dreamer*
is parked along the road, a Mexican family barbequing
pork & sausage with children twirling happily nearby.
The father looks up as I pass, smiles. Sometimes
all you need is a good dream to guide, regardless of borders,
privilege. The quotient of despair rises among the rich
with every expectation met: what could be more frightening
than nothing new to satisfy?

Allah's Garden

Riding along the Pacific, I pass a Muslim family
picnicking in a grove of Monterey Pine.
The daughters have beautiful faces, no veils—
elaborate cloth adorning them from crown to sole.
The father, devout, kneels on a burgundy Persian carpet,
bowing towards Mecca. Along the beach,
women with more skin than clothes turn their bodies
toward sun, its own kind of worship. How long

before two worlds collide, burn; or we,
discern in every contrast a flagrant beauty—
each face another shade of God?

Where the Grass Is Greener Still

The Holiday Inn Express room window peers out
over the Lincoln-Mercury car dealership, but there is green
everywhere beyond. The green of lush Indiana forests,
the green of meadows, thick foliage, the green of neighborhood lawns
stretching across acres that mowers huge as tractors dutifully cut
in long, neat rows.

The Ford mini-vans, Dodge Ram trucks with their huge, gleaming grills
stride across the landscape as Roman chariots, emblems of a new empire,
just as thirsty.

Row upon row of red brick houses shelter the blue-collar husbands,
silent & noble in their baseball caps and close-cropped hair,
something royal in their manner, the way basketball is coached
as a sacrament, the way children are shaped, bent, poured
into molds tough as the brick that surrounds, the way
beer is buried by the boxful in basement refrigerators—
a buffer, a bomb shelter, the toll brave deeds of living exact.

Upstairs, wives roam the hallways & bedrooms devout in the faith
there is no other life than this—that children are the center,
that husbands live in little league, in weekend work, in private basements,
that Mother Mary receives their secret prayers: will forgive the final sin
of never being enough.

The children rise each morning, point their eyes ahead as race-horses
ridden from the starting-blocks, blinders fixing their gaze on the goal:
        an American life. As with most empires,
what to do once you've won is what nags, what gnaws—
every car in the lot roaring its engine, hungry for road,
for the bend in the road, for what cannot be seen
in the green of wide lawns.

A Rose, a Thorn

Watching *Shakespeare In Love* with my daughter, about love,
its betrayal, and how does one explain. Passion's vagaries:
the wilted rose, the bruised fruit—in its season, the bloom,
the blush. Much remains the same,

as in old England's time: whole continents shifting
in the small space of the heart. A single glance or brush
of fingertip, then as now, wilts the body with heat,
the white heat of electrical storm, the distance between
heaven & earth shortened to the length of a breath, a lip.
But can she comprehend,

vaster than the Atlantic's wide basin, the distance between
the woman she may become & the women who first stepped
on these shores? After a few years: wedding bells sounding
as the dull clank about a cow's neck, the fine sheen of young
skin burnished stiff as furniture, a life chosen by father,
by husband. Only later,

across a vast continent of kitchen tables, legs trembling
from tremors rippling beneath every foundation, one woman
after another pushing back her chair, peering into the eyes
of the man across that table, taking what was hers. A rose,
a basket of fruit: to *be* the gardener, the one who clips the stem,
offers the petal & the thorn, the one who sucks the juice
from the pulp down to the marrow of seed. This

gift my daughter ponders, as the movie credits slip across
the screen as a stream of years, not so far removed from this
Shakespearean stage where the only players were men—pretending
the cry of birth, the lament of death, every sound between. Nothing
shields her from what is hers: this prick of thorn, her petal bruised,
this tangle of root growing beneath secret ground—and in its season,
her blush, her bloom.

A Pearl Of Great Price

Tulsa, Oklahoma fades into dusk
from my eleventh-story window at the Ramada,
a hotel that must once have been new, shiny—like America—
but now, rust pours from the bathtub spout, the hairdryer
falls off the wall, the air-conditioner laments all night long,
and the pink door to my room is chipped, ugly. Below
in the streets, I walk and hardly see a soul, broken brick
along the downtown mall catching my shoe every few paces,
empty office space waiting for someone, anyone—restaurants
sullenly open with handfuls of patrons scattered here and there.
Not a movie theater in sight, as though there were no longer a story
to tell, except for the churches and banks, steeple and skyscraper
vying for height, for the right to save your money, your soul.
I know there is a secret life here, obvious to its citizens, rooted
in a depth no tourist can see. But I wonder,

is this how the British felt, their far-flung empire in India,
the Americas, shrinking to small isles. Or Rome, towards the end,
those famous roads and frescoes overrun by restless hordes
eager to live their own way. It all can shift in a minute—
and even when it has, nobody knows for years, not right away,
how the tide has turned, that their season is past, that what you've been
hoarding all this time will be gathered, eventually, by another. This,
then, a prayer:

that we shall all inherit the earth—a little here, a little there—
that when the new king-makers of corporation and conglomerate
move their riches, again, we will not care, knowing
a secret life is always inside us, waiting—
can never be taken away

as dusk becomes night, and the lights blink on
all across town as silver pearls
in a black sea.

What Does It Mean To Be Safe At Home?

The rain falls and falls, then goes.
The sun gleams on the spread of green lawn,
Reds of Cincinnati falling prey to Pirates from Pittsburgh,
long balls floating through sky as pigeons carrying messages,
secret wars muscled behind every bat, every mitt. We sink
with every missed swing, win with every base gained—
it is genetic, the long spears spiraling through air
to the heart of prey, the hard clubs beating away
what threatens home.

The balls fall and fall, then we go.
Hunting for small victories down along the freeways,
we invent what cannot be found. Everyone needs a story
to make it through. This is enough to take home.
It has been a long day, a long millennium or two.

Red pirates fill my dreams at night,
streaming from dugouts. I am falling & falling
through one error after another, dropping balls everywhere—
people argue fair or foul, fat men in black suits insist I'm safe,
but I feel bruised, dirty. It's okay, they say, *you're home.*

Hubris

A parade down Main Street in Madison, Indiana.
Tons of machinery, John Deere tractors large as dinosaurs
pulling wooden floats draped with American flags, young girls
in sequin gowns, hands waving like the queen, middle-aged men
all smiles, perched with beer and cigarettes on lumbering trailers
carrying hydro-planes, each powered by a single aircraft engine,
covered with a sleek red, green, yellow plastic body sleek as a jet fighter,
pulled behind equally huge diesel trucks capable of pulling a house,
or a lie.

A succession of smiling fat men ride by, bodies stuffed
inside tiny go-cart sized racing cars, or astride miniature motorbikes
no bigger than tricycles, golden tasseled hats whipping in the wind
as they veer along the parade route doing circle 8's, shrieking to a stop
in front of laughing children's toes. Shriners, Masons, Elk, Moose
dressed in red sashes, elaborate swords dawdling beneath bellies
curved as sand dunes, mystical rites infusing the boredom
of small town jobs with an importance every king
lusts for.

I forge a golden armor, arrogance roaring its engines louder
than any hydro-plane, something in me already lost.
What fashions this blindness, this gray mirror,
this inability to see a different beauty, quivering in the dusk
as smoke rising from streets where everyone knows
your first name.

Engine

The Los Gatos parking lot is filled with Lexus,
PT Cruisers, & Hummers. Housewives angular & tan
stream by, eyelids creamed & lined, optimistic breasts
nonchalantly pointing straight ahead, past the men
striding confidently with their cell phones
plugged to ears as though listening to somebody's gospel,
or mutual funds rising, or another country falling.
Emerging, then disappearing again inside sleek metal
& fiberglass cocoons, pistons fire in each cylinder of heart,
spinning the world's crankshaft, powering this endless rotation
through the void. There is always

someplace to go, something new to want.
And the young single women slide by so unencumbered,
radiant, untested by weddings, births, the thought of death—
engines humming beneath hips, cache of eggs to spill or grow.
How the young men revel, penises purring under red hoods,
bent on roaring down the road. Or the aging beauty in pink pants,
blue star shimmering on the curve of each bouncing cheek—
doesn't someone love her like a secret, like the only one
worth having? Sometimes

there's just too much speed, something in you careening,
looking for more, always more, cylinders of the heart
wanting to slow, to meander past these opulent hills
into the great brown fields of the San Joaquin—
so much space you almost feel lonely for the small
huddled towns, could almost start again—odometer
counting down the years, the ones that are left,
numerals fluttering languidly towards zero.

Destinations Unknown

Reading about guns, germs, steel—the fate
of human societies. How Cro-Magnon used their superior flint
to destroy the Neanderthals, who actually had the bigger brain,
knew how to bury their dead, care for the sick. Then in Polynesia,
the peaceful Moriori slaughtered by a handful of Maori farmers
skilled at war—always, the more advanced destroying
the simpler.

Of course now, we as virulent seeds from Europe are blown
everywhere across the globe, flowering as weeds, muscling
the roots of the indigenous. When Pizarro's small band
of soldiers defeated 80,000 Inca warriors at Cajamarca,
one world ended, another began. This is how
it has always been.

How tender, then, the face of the militia child tucked away
in Idaho hill or rough Wyoming terrain. The father, setting his rifle
ready against the porch, peers through binoculars
down the crumbling cavern, waiting for something to come.
When it does, what then will we say?
Who will have been saved?

Breakfast On the Haight

The post-modern hippies look almost the same
as they did, here, in the sixties along Haight-Ashbury—
torn blue jeans, love tattoos, psychedelic clothes.
But these days, beside them in line at the People's Café,
a clean-cut family with two blond children, oblivious
to the irony. All of us in the café, at home in a world
that has changed just this much.

Altered States Of America

At the People's Café on Haight—
after dropping children at the airport early,
then napping in our car at Golden Gate park—
I stare at my table filled with coffee beans under glass,
then at a store front with psychedelic sun, moon,
high priestess painted between carved pillars, remember
life as a place of worship, a temple of love, see it
in the eyes of store-keepers unlocking padlocked gates,
sweeping sidewalks clean—who look me in the eye,
say hello. After all these years, a breeze still flurries
the leaves of tall trees along the street,
as a calypso song on the café's radio intones
~wake-up, wake-up~
and for long rapturous moments
~open your eyes, open your eyes~
I know what being American was supposed to mean.

Radar

There was a man
unraveling down the sidewalk along
    the backside of the Capitol's Rotunda
a man vexed
      all in a wrangle
   arm through a tattered vet jacket
  holding a black phone receiver
  talking loud trying to get through
  to somebody...
but it was an old 50's phone
frayed cord dangling from the mouthpiece--
      it wasn't connected
    and no-one was listening.

There was a woman
whimsical and wiry as a homeless gypsy
  worn red jacket and yellow scarves
  radiating so bright
  she'd be impossible to miss
unless that was your plan
     smiled as I passed
  caught that glint in my eye like
    a hidden wavelength
     called out behind me
   How are you today? Yes you, you look alive!
and I am and wonder
    how she knows...
    an invisible beam
   emanating between agents
   secret in the wrong country.

There were three cadets
young white and true blue jogging by
     in grey shorts neatly cut hair
      innocent and clean as the sons
    you're supposed to have
  chuckling between easy breaths
     eyes like radar
   scanning for what is out of place
on their tracking screens
        light on we other three
circling the capitol looking
    for a way in,   and I
wondering will we show up
  as friend or foe.

Sweet Trivia

My son wanders over to my lap, explains
the drawings on his hand-made birthday announcement,
how *Sponge-Bob Square-pants* is inviting everyone to his party—
and I marvel, unable to fathom the strange beauty of this boy,
clasp him across my lap, refuse to let go. Until my daughter
begins calling out history trivia from the bedroom,
how Sir Francis Drake was a pirate, took gold & silver bullion
from the Spanish armada despite its 130 ships, 30,000 men &
2,400 cannon. She wonders why she needs to know
the endless drudgery of history's detail when so young,
but confesses the wars are enthralling, has no explanation
for this.

Meanwhile, my wife recounts her trip to New York,
the hotel Millennium opening onto the stubborn rubble
of missing towers, and she, unable to fathom the strange beauty
of the unnumbered who, dust into dust, circle in the air,
refuse to let go. Of course,
        there is no explanation, really, for any of it:
what we keep hold of, what must be let go. Just now,
I could find endless reasons for running from the unexplainable
detail of the world—but have only to slide down
the silica of neural pathways splaying through the body
of a boy in square pants, a girl whose soul is already full
of bittersweet paradox, to know why I stay—

the world unfolding its extravagant trivia,
the unfathomable odds that amid armada, oil, gun
we are here, still—mulling every bitter fact,
every sweet particular.

Of Wood and Steel

My son cleans the deck with me,
our rusted saws plunging like swords
between the cracks of redwood board,
rooting out the past year's fall of dead
olive leaves, our dog's thick malamute husky fur.

Debris lines the empty spaces, clogging the airways,
the wood unable to breath—like the choked stairwells
of those twin towers shivering in the morning air
as rugged behemoths oblivious to impending collapse,
how the detritus of incinerated steel would clog the arteries
of Manhatten, white dust falling as snow
into the cracks of everything.

These old saws are rusted, but the jagged teeth
bite and claw through what is dead in the hope
old boards will last a little longer. My son
soon tires, lays down his tool, walks inside to play—
plunging a small airplane, into the tall leggo tower
saying *this is what happened dad, just like this.*

I nod assent, turn back with blistered hand
still trying to separate what has grown together,
the wood, the dust, lives seeping in beneath skin,
beneath hope, into cracks everywhere.

Emergency Procedures

They search my wife, running the metal detector
over the length of her body, unable to find
what we later knew: it was the wire in her bra.
The wooden knitting needles are found,
too like a hijacker weapon to let on board.
Walking past the camouflaged soldiers in the lobby,
my children are afraid, despite all reassurance:
the many small ways war touches us,
the mundane, the personal.

Nestled firm in the coach seat,
my leather jacket affords the illusion
I am a soldier of sorts, ready for anything,
protected from nothing. I look for things to do.
The no cigarette sign is easy. Fasten my belt.
Push an overhead button, light streams down. I scan
the laminated emergency procedures folded neatly
in the seat pocket. The hidden yellow oxygen mask,
life-vest under the cushion, inflatable rafts stowed away,
flotation devices everywhere,
    useless
over land, over sea—but totems nonetheless, promises
my children eagerly review every plane trip.

Each destination poses a question: where have we come to?
At least the motels try to answer, the Gideon Bible
in every drawer as a map—but who travels that way anymore?
The Vedas, the Talmud, the Koran: full of prayer and war,
always, a Holy War. Maps to the wrong place,
yet we arrive again.

Finally, we touch down at our destination. My young son,
conscious now of gravity, the plane's, the world's,
turns with his fists in the air, smiling
    we survived, we survived!

46

That night, I search the news for what just happened,
what could happen, what will happen without
a new compass, a new map, a new way of getting there.

What We Have To Offer

A mountain is a mountain,
not a commentary on my life,
so the zen parable says. But war
looms ahead, again—everything at once
speaking to me, even the mountains, the tunnels
below Afghanistan where *devils* live, defiant,
like the dark angels swooning in the black heart
of my country, aghast.

We have been deceived.
It can all happen to us, every last terror.
Beneath the rubble of each gleaming spire,
something was incinerated.

Could it be what separates you from me?

Or is each gaping hole a double helix,
the genetics of revenge: each eye, each tooth,
each severed hand all we have to offer,
all we have to claim?

What We Cannot See

A red Coca-Cola can lays empty in the sand—
splintered hole from an Afghan carbine tumbling
the aluminum sacrament from its perch on the baked rock.
Target practice, ambivalent icon—longed for, forbidden.

Parched lips are teased by visions of black liquid,
effervescent, electric—western devils mixing with virgins
in some promised land, but which one? The afterlife
bears strong resemblance to television, desire
beckoning, sated, spawning. Everything with a hole in it:
flags, buildings, yearning.

A world away, I sip chai, wonder what I would give
my life for, am I giving it away now, to what end.
There is a squandered heaven, here, on earth.
I live among the few with enough to hoard.
Which is why hands beat at every door,
wanting in.

I am afraid to look in the mirror, assuming halos,
fearing horns. What we cannot see haunts us.

There is a world outside every bolted door,
waiting to open.

Behemoth

"(*The United States) is complicated, paradoxical, bullheaded,*
shy, cruel, boisterous, unspeakably dear, and very beautiful."
—John Steinbeck
Waters cover the earth.
Our bodies flow with desire, more liquid than bone.
This is the tempest inside skin, craving's conduit: water of semen,
water of birth, human storm in a womb. Born in red of blood, white
fear, blue sea—crossing in storm, carrying storm, becoming the storm
that would lay waste a continent, as buffalo tongues lapping great rivers
of water, lapping the vast plains of wilderness under boot.
Rifle, beard, blood in water—stampeding as a single beast,
a behemoth shimmering in dust, glorious, stained. Here,

upon the bones of ancient people, a new world rises
from the ash of another, always another, staggers, lurches about—
limbs curling into the pattern of wheels, of covered wagon,
locomotive, great turbine engines of industry laid upon land
as a grid, lit, telegraphed—Europe's seed teeming,
Africa's sweat, and Asia's toiling—a great creature emerging,
driven, ingenious, unabashed, pulling from itself the steamboat,
the reaper, the steel plow, electric lamp, telephone. Then airplane,
assembly line—cruel industry, wondrous science, shimmering capital
converging in holy triumvirate to birth radio, television, movies,
the moon reached, the kiss of medicine, field of plastics, electronics,
energy of oil, of radium, X-ray, computer, the human genome mapped,
waiting. Now,

we have the world's attention. So we've won—
have we nothing better to offer than merchandise?
The grail of blue jeans, the siren call of fast food,
the glittering cavern of warehouse rows aglow
with toothpaste, sneakers, the holy roll-call of name-brand—
teasing the many with what can only belong to few.

Freedom, and this is what we choose: appetite
as a feather in the stomach, seductive, irritable—
the seven seas roiling in a storm of want, an aching tide,
and always, a new land to pity, enroll, harvest.
Was it only a dream,

this instinct to preserve, a roar of hooves
so plentiful across the wide plains
the throat catches in grief: that such beauty could be.
All of us, nuzzling the earth as a new-born,
feeding the world from our own body,
every country a long lost cousin,
tails flicking in a stretch of afternoon sun,
standing on wobbly legs or sure, cacophony
of different voices braying as a single sound,
contented, hopeful. But now

the headlines roar a different story,
of ice-caps melting, the threat of another war,
the ennui of tabloid gossip, the patriotic call
to spend again & again, to open our mouths wide,
saying nothing, swallowing everything. If this
is what we are, then who will save us
from what is truly hungry in the world: another beast
born of our neglect, reflected in waters of want rising,
rising as a tide—so many standing fierce in the rain,
a tempest inside skin, a human storm,
a reckoning.

This American Life

It could be   Roman, Aztec, the reign of Huns—
there have been so many, glittering empires whose patrons
know nothing of the shadow their long banners cast. Who
remembers the lost? The language of captives is secret,
a history of prayer more than history itself—whose pages
are written, always, by victors.

Those who win may remember their own, row upon row
of soldiers silent in their noble helmets, something brave
in their manner, the way war is received as a sacrament,
youth a harvest, the way the enemy is bent, broken,
poured into stories reminiscent of sport:

the final showdown, the last stand. The way we recline
in easy chairs too drunk with triumph to know
what was lost. The way sons, friends are returned
to rest beneath the broad green fields, lives fumbled
into obscurity. There is something in the way

skin color shades what you see, the jerseys of red & white,
of blue & black, the gleaming helmets of opponents,
of lions & rams, of patriots & cowboys, the way one man
must have more than his neighbor because he can,
the extra yard of dirt, the daring leap over the pile
into the end zone, the last man standing, finally, alone.
There is something in the way

ivy destroys a tree, appearing at first like love, the clamor
of limbs to entangle, to surround, the struggle of ascent,
the proliferation of foliage green as thin dollars tightening
round trunk & root, seducing drop by drop the affection
of moisture, till what was loved stands dry, a husk, brittle
as tinder. There is always something

in the way—the world glittering as a trophy for the strong;
for the rest, the struggle in the pile beneath.

I Am a White Man

"What's going on in your country…The only stories
  and poems we read that tell us anything about everyday life
  in the United States come from the blacks,the Latinos,
  the Asian Americans…Others, the whites, the majority…
  their writing often seems so disconnected from the country's
  problems…Why are American writers so coded…so private?"
          — pg. 10, Al Young's preface to Ploughshares
              "Believers" edition, Spring 1993.

I am not a black man.
But I know there are things wrong with this country.
I am not a Chinese American woman.
But there is a voice in me that knows the truth.
I am not a Latino, or mestizo peasant.
But I am wondering about my place in this land they once owned.

The new century circles around our lives
like an eagle or a vulture, and I cannot tell which,
yet.

I am a white man.
I am the green of Ireland.
I am the scarlet of English soldiers.
I am the Swedish grandfather…white with winters,
a stowaway aboard a ship sailing to a land of dreams.

I am a white man
whose heart is hidden
by masks of privilege,
by indecipherable codes lifting me
above glass ceilings.

But stones are thrown
at the glass above us all.

I am a white man
who extends an open hand,
with a heart that once beat innocent
as every child in every womb in every mother
of every color.

I am a white man
who dreams that rainbow after the storm:
bridge from one place to another.
I am color blazing across the sky
after the rains have ended—
even this reign of white.

Spectrum

i.
Between woman and man there is color—
the red of vein,
the white of bone,
the green of eye,
the blue of heart—
more the same than not.

ii.
In the shades between
brown & white, black, yellow
red—more color than we know
waits to be born; who then
will we be?

iii.
There is a color shared
between white collar and blue,
hands leathered like saddle or suede—
when cut, bleed the same—
the red of fathers,
the red of mothers.

iv.
In the end, there is one color,
more absence than hue,
buried dark in earth & night,
becomes the husk, the seed,
the light.

Norte Americano

We have arrived at the end of the earth, cannibalizing
the four directions, everything that lies between.

There is no end to what we cannot have, which is what we want;
every king knows this—the world is not enough.

Hunger consumes its children, picks over the bones that remain.
We are the children of bones, oblivious to what consumes us.

We are loud.

Silence has many advantages—hearing what we cannot have,
the open hand, the space it leaves, the nothing that is left

our one hope, emptiness capable of receiving, what is simple:

the heft of a hoe handle,
the weight of water

a fist uncurling fingers

surrendering this infinite seduction, the chain of want
spread across the globe as a cloud, pale as the skin of ghosts.

Omens

South of Limon on the Caribbean coast of Costa Rica
there were voices,
        I was not mad, though it is difficult to tell
when you are up against a wall and don't know it
something needs to break through, the voice of the great deep,
so why not a god or angel or demon, this time
it was the need to change my life, unequivocally,
so the signs came, walking alone down an endless beach,
the rhythmical waves collapsing, resurrecting again and again,
the bluewhite sky shouting its long silence,
the soft mesh of salt water sand endlessly receiving me,
each palm leaf waving, waving for my attention,
but I was deaf, blind, often dumb, which is why
this body groans so, each pain the first brush strokes
of some lethal art working on heart, skin, limbic system.
I must have needed more than this morning's alarm,
even this deliriously loud day to turn me around,
so there it came ambling along the beach, a dog
loping in the opposite direction, a massive albino
with my name, a Great Dane, pale as I,
oblivious, running the wrong way—it wasn't enough
to change me, just a bit of humor the gods send now and then
to amuse themselves in a Jungian way—but I was lucky,
the occasional second chance came roaring from behind,
the sound of hooves, the kicking up of salt foam wave,
four great horses carrying four brown men,
dreadlocked hair flapping as flags of a better country,
torn khakis, bare chests, bearing the promise of a life
just good enough to be enough—riding past
this life of too much that is never enough.

Leaning Towards The Southern Hemisphere

Samara, Costa Rica

Veranda, hammock—refuge from what I'd become.
Small red frogs with immense toes sit silent
in trees nearby, poisonous, bearing witness. Forgetting myself,
I worship every cocoanut husk, green parrot, afternoon rain.
Even mosquitoes sound like singing, feel like tiny bruised kisses.
All insolence drains from my body, reverence the only tongue I know.

There is something here: milk inside the husk.
Beneath the ground, a single bean germinates.

Inside the bean, the husk, a mountain grows:
it is my life.

Full Moon In Costa Rica

It began with mosquito bites, fifty-one on her arm alone.
Eighty-seven covering his small white body—skin ripe
as bruised fruit. Children are food for many things.

Red welts spring up like tiny volcanoes in snow.
Like the earth, my children are young, only shrug.

Traveling from this world to another, one moves
from gold to rust and back—unsure which is which.

It is the oldest religion:
tongues of parents praying for their young.
There are many things to fear, to love.

*

The Alfarro Empressa bus terminal, voices swelling
as in a dream you can't understand, doors that begin roads
to places you may not intend to see—but need to find.
Unknown friends, amigos step forward—we pantomime
a muted play: luggage, ticket seat.

The man with no smile, moving steadily
down the aisle collecting tickets, and we,
Americanos lost without one, then found
at the last moment in pocket—belonging again.
The sight—a bus, twin to ours,
impaled on the road by a Jeep Cherokee sunk
halfway into its front—a family with children
still crushed in their seats. Fellow passengers
peer out the windows as we move on, our bus
passing slower vehicles round curves same as before.

The long wait—our bus stranded in the road,
driver tinkering endlessly with the motor.
A bright-eyed couple share fruit with us in the field nearby.
My children's eyes ask at each new sight:
Is this how it is, is this how things are supposed to happen?
I think: there is no supposed to, only what is.

*

Later that night, we pull into Samara along the Pacific coast,
manage to find a flat-bed truck for a taxi, load ourselves
into the back for the short-ride to the beach, to our room:
Las Brisas Del Pacifico.

Under a full moon we swim, eat, end with chocolate *helado*,
the cream thick. I am a devotee, unsure of the proper tongue,
even to whom I am addressing each breath as long syllabled prayers.

Fear is scripture anyone can recite. But love, that is a different verse.

Ah, companero, what shall we sing tonight,
under this shimmering moon?

One World

In San Francisco, the Zen waiters at the sushi dive bring bacon & eggs
twenty-four hours a day. I sit at late breakfast, meditate over the paper,
the national guardsman in Afghanistan saying *You get to see places
tourists never do. We're like tourists with guns.* A man in black beret,
blue work-shirt, sits at my table, borrows the front page. We too are
tourists, a kind of soldier savaging the morning headlines for stories,
for the secret thrill of catastrophe and chaos civilized by the black
& white of newsprint without the smell of blood. His phone rings,
sleek and silver as a bullet, and he's off to more important news—the
private, the personal, the privilege of a life immune to the vagaries
of warlords and famine, this *First World* hegemony, Eisenhower's
corporate-war complex—and you know, when warned by a president
that your world is no longer *your* world, but the playground of CEO's
with guns, then it might be time to believe that *they* believe that the
rest of this world must be kept a *Third World* for the few in the world
who matter. This is what I was thinking, dipping the strip of bacon
into yellow yoke—the inescapable violence, the snorting pig, the hen's
unborn children, the way our hands are stained with blood whichever
way we turn—but how the story must turn, somewhere, if it is to be
a good story, one that any true god would read—hidden somewhere
in the next chapter, lurking in a paragraph one had almost given up
hope of stumbling upon—the one where we, as tourists in our own
country, as soldiers of this *One World,* point the guns of our hearts
at the tyranny of this story gone bad, this American Dream for the
few, the privileged—squeeze the trigger of our deepest prayers, *fire!*

Grateful Deadheads Talk Trash At the Café

They remind me of any group of corner tavern drinkers, brash & inflated, opinions falling from tongues like foam-headed cappuccino or lager, syllables spread round the room like so much smoke, crudely erudite & gruff all at the same time, how we love to hear ourselves talk, making the world by saying so, no matter the clique, the zealotry, it's all in the speaking, like now,

young hippie wanna-be's posing as Tibetan-bag toting, tie-dye orange-purple shirted caterers of swank wine auctions, holding temp jobs as undercover security dressed like *the normals,* keeping an eye on the light-fingered, slipping thousand dollar bottles of cabernet under coat and making for the door. Now, the morning after, it's all about the misshapen bodies of the rich, their plump children, bellies and thighs lumbering dangerously in stretch nylon or baggy cotton, it's all a plot, they are the ones, the cause of the world's undeniably predicated end, doesn't matter

where you go, southern Baptist land or northwest cultured cool, sweet LA oxygen bar or corner barber stool, it's always the same, always *them,* spoken with curl of lip, almost a spit, doesn't matter who they are, as long as it's clear it's not *us*—the rich fucks who rule the world, the righteous billion to whom it's owed, the pentagon patsies, grateful dead head lackeys, republican racketeers with their oil & steers, democratic dopes, loggers on the ropes, protestor pinheads afraid to pull the trigger, patriotic mass-murderers with the itchy nuclear fingers—it's always them, the reason for the madness, 'cuz if everyone was just like me, shit, things would be a whole lot better.

Failure To Notice the Signs

After the movie about oil and torture
in the Middle East, I return past midnight
to the parking lot where rows of cars
had been. The tow-truck driver revs
his huge flat-bed like a demon,
wheels round, cinches the last vehicle
on-board. Flicking his fading cigarette
as I approach to find my car, I ruminate
on torture, picture him drenched in oil,
a single ember falling, torching his big
ball-bearings—instead, take his card,
make arrangements for the morning.
The whole damn thing could fall apart—
jihad, holy war, the American way—
and maybe we'd be better off. Rows
of bicycles, armies of feet pedaling
towards the future. Windmill wings
rotating across vast hills, rows of silver
panels reflecting solar light. Or maybe
we'll all simply fall, back into darkness
without the black gold that runs invisible
in the veins of each computer, tire, appliance—
feeding civilization, the engine of commerce,
the lubricant of a global economy
slick as the smile of the tow-truck driver
crushing his cigarette in the asphalt
with his boot, climbing into his diesel cab,
roaring into the night with the last car
on the lot.

Alternative Evangelism

Parked on the street: a gray Toyota,
ancient, every inch covered with bumper stickers.
The driver rests on curbside bench adjacent,
snoozing behind dark glasses, wearing a black hat,
black leather jacket, black shirt, black pants,
sporting a gray beard, brown cane, turquoise ring.
I peruse this poet's vehicular manuscript, see
Mini-vans are tangible evidence of Evil, wince
at the sight of my old Plymouth Voyager
parked across the way—relate more to
Keep the Books, Burn the Censors, and
Somewhere in Texas there's a village missing an idiot,
though years hence folks will have forgotten
that burning bush. Then of course, the perennial
Taxes Suck and the new *What's our oil doing under their soil?*
Though I don't take kindly to the burning of books,
I do listen now to the burning bushes on the torched earth
of our latest little war, believe in the bumper-sticker
Honor the Dead, Respond with Peace, and
One People, One Planet, One Future. But just as I'm
about to have my own little religious revival,
the poet in dark glasses rises from his bench,
ambles back to his parked poem of a car,
climbs behind the wheel and steers down the street—
a wandering evangelist half advertisement,
half sacred text, at least half as good
and half as right as all the prophets
that have come before. As he turns
the corner, the last prophecy I spy
shimmering on silver bumper in sun is
Mommy, what were trees like?

Patriotism

Deep in the heartland visiting family,
I step from the shower, reach for a towel,
find myself draped in the flag: red & white stripes
longer than torso, than feet & fingers can stretch,
the blue field of fifty stars rubbing against chest, abdomen,
skin that is private, skin that is public. For a moment,

I fear two things: that a Kentucky state police car
will screech to a halt in front of the house with siren
& lights blazing, dragging me to the local station for desecrating
an American flag. Or secondly, that California's counter-culture
secret service will jump from the bushes and drag me home
to the redwoods—interrogating me along the way in a beat-up
Volkswagen van about the political incorrectness of wrapping
myself so snugly in this ultimate symbol of corporate, capitalist
hegemony. Of course,

I assure myself that *you're not paranoid if they really are after you!*
so continue to dry toe & ear, belly & shoulder—wondering
at the world's 475 billionaires whose combined income is more
than the bottom half of everyone else, each an empire that would
rival old England, Spain or Portugal, dwarf the French, even
the Chinese. Feeling glum about being a *have-not*, I remember
my own modest life—a home, two vehicles 10 years old,
a computer, a guitar, a few trips here & there—places me
in the upper 5% of the entire world's population. I am a *have*,
afterall. But now I'm starting to sweat,

the towel absorbing more than my brain, this business of being
middle-class taking on a new dimension, caught not in some middle
purgatory between Bill Gates, the Rockefellers, and the rest
of India's minions, Africa's millions—but firmly in an upper tier I was
unaware of belonging to. *What am I supposed to do with this information!*
intones Holly Hunter's character in *Living Out Loud*, besieged
in her kitchen by the relentlessness of the world's news pummeling

her till she knew: *you must change your life*. This was Rilke's conclusion,
standing in front of Apollo's archaic torso, the glimpse of a perfect
human form ending all possibility of living

anything less. By now, I am dry—Kentucky in-laws wondering
what this west-coast poet could be doing so long in the bathroom.
I emerge draped in the colors that made us: the blue of heart,
the white of privilege, the red of blood. Knowing this time,
it will take every flag of every color, no-one left behind.

Dark Flowers Speaking

Dark Flowers Speaking

For Afghan poet Nadia Anjuman

They say poetry has no power, sitting as a limp flower in a vase. But when the Taliban fell, Nadia was still beaten to death by her husband, by her own mother, for her verse. *Gul-e-dodi—Dark Flower*, her poem-petals a dangerous way of loving. In this hour, I spy in the great fields of my own country, countless black roses opening, speaking.

Why Men In Wartime Are Not To Be Trusted

Prince Eugene of Sweden rides with a German officer during World War I, who quotes the poet Holderlin as they travel a wintry forest road. Up ahead, a captive Russian soldier buried to his waist in snow is made to point directions in the dusky light. At the next turn, another soldier, guiding arm outstretched, and then another. The prince is concerned the men will die of cold, but the officer says not to worry, they are already dead—shot and planted in the snow, frozen arms outstretched to show the way.

Who Could Dream Such Horrible Beauty?

A thousand cavalry horses, fleeing enemy fire, flounder into a Finnish lake on the very night it freezes over for the winter. In the morning, the lake appears as a vast sheet of white marble on which rest hundreds of horse's heads, glistening like broken statuary on a grand chessboard.

**Both poems inspired by stories in Kaputt, by Curzio Malaparte*

The War To End All Wars

Russian prisoners were separated into those who could read and those who couldn't, so the educated could be massacred. One hundred thousand German women were raped by Russian soldiers during the occupation, suicide a survival strategy, or hoping for an officer who brings food, wine. Even dogs were trained to carry explosives under armored cars and blow themselves up. After all this, the trumpets still blare, the red rockets glare, the bombs bursting in air.

The Battle For Our Hearts

The radio in the airport-shuttle blares *2,000 American soldiers dead in Iraq*. The man across from me huffs that we lost 10,000 a day in World War II, so what's the big deal? The shuttle quiets as the news continues its loud ordeal, rebel forces exploding their own bodies to force America out—the man says again *they should all be shot*. Next to me, his Asian friend offers *I don't agree, let's find out why they're doing it*, as several passengers of ethnic descent quietly nod their heads. The man, exasperated, blurts *I don't care why!* Which is the reason for the dead—theirs, ours—feeding the earth with silent questions, answers germinating like dark seeds in our hearts.

War

Navy ships in the bay near Vallejo,
reminding me of father in Korea,
uncle Bob near Japan. What death
they saw—how they struggled
to live after. That is one ship
I will never board,
though the world cry
to arms, again, to arms!

Motivation

In New York, a mother kneels
next to her son's baby carriage,
points to the torn sidewalk,
the street unearthed—gargantuan
yellow cranes consuming concrete.
How the great machines of civilization
bite and tear at the ground,
remove what is broken,
manufacture a safer world.
In other buildings, generals & terrorists
plot acceptable levels of carnage.
But the young boy, eyes wide,
gasps, claps his hands—
as though it was all being done
just for him.

Everyman

After the London subway bombings,
police chased a new suspect onto a train,
shooting him five times in front of horrified passengers.
Hours later, police released grainy photographs
of four more would-be bombers as they boarded
three subway trains and a red double-decker bus.
The newspaper stated

their apparent ordinariness was striking.
When the police commissioner asked a nation
do you recognize any of these men? I peered
into the mirror, into my deep ordinariness,
and said *yes*.

No Surrender

It's difficult to write of war: the blaming, the bombs. How buildings
are obliterated, but sometimes a stand of trees remain—or a soldier
can't help but hold an orphaned puppy found in rubble. It's difficult
to explain what we live with: the dead bodies, the way we let it go
on. War comes so easily: the pain inside—feel it lift, point, threaten.

Something In Us

The weekend army reserve soldiers marooned in Iraq
longer than imagined, asked to soften-up the prisoners
by stripping them down to leashes, panties—
then piling them naked together in a heap.
But it was the smiles, the *thumbs-up!*
from captors wishing only for home that appalled—
so many of us, uncomprehending the ways of empire.
How in the name of freedom, you can do anything
to anybody and still believe.

A Prayer For Less

Standing on a bridge, looking at white puff-ball whiffs
falling through the air. In my hand, a folded newspaper:
faces and names of all the soldiers killed in Iraq
staring up at me. Oil is a dangerous need.
To send sons, and now daughters, to war for this—
the wind lifting each life into the air, and, try as I might,
failing to catch a single one.

Rainy Morning

The morning paper is covered in cellophane, protecting the delicate pulp from tears at the news. A fallen soldier honored, local boy— three rounds of gunfire, three boxes of doves to end the funeral. The Humvee, the roadside bomb, the desert country as far now as heaven from this grey morning—and our war-making unabated, festering.

Enough

I reach into the small brown paper bag for a cranberry muffin, see the story buried on the paper's back page, and am undone. Sometimes I cannot find the separation from the world I need to go on. And so, I am still hungry in Sudan, a prostitute in Malaysia, a warlord in Iraq—fearing the day America will have no more use for me, will have had enough.

The Weather In Our Hearts

Ice storms at Christmas from Canada to the Texas panhandle—
all flights to the Midwest canceled. Retreating home, I
review the weather map in the paper, and of course, there
is so much more to see. Map of war, map of hunger, map of
human contradiction: this fight for peace, always, the same fight.

Another Christmas Story

The stars over Bethlehem, still clouded by smoke. Mecca, encircled
by soldiers. The fertile triangle flowing with black gold. Generals
talk, divide the world with corporate behemoths: not a wise man
among them.

Oil will go the way of myrrh & frankincense: an old story to tell of
the past. Perhaps then it will be water, or air: the invaluable, rare
gift. Who then will die for our sins?

In someone's body—or an ear of corn in Kansas, or floating on the
Dead Sea—are the molecules of the first child to be born in a world
without war. Is there a prophet among us brave enough to believe?

Absent War's Preoccupations

Five men descend
the steep pathless mountainside,
backs heavy with packs, straight down
scraggle of granite & manzanita,
over cliff ledges till the ground finally curves,
rounding into the small valley.
We straggle happy & exhausted
into the tall grove of pine, nestle
tents & gear next to the river,
rummage dead twigs, dry leaves—
then later, round fire old as men
begin again to gnaw the bone:
this mystery of wives, children
wounding us deeper with love
than ever imagined. How
age affects desire, growing
deeper in some directions,
less urgent in others. Sex,
work, money—sniffing for
the god in each, measuring
the balance of sacrifice
& payoff, and when
does the heart know
if you've settled for too little,
paid too much? Who knew
that men, absent weapons,
could be so essential
to survival?

Small Dreams

I walk past a church at noon with its twelve bell tolls,
wonder why it is we do what we do, war looming again,
absurd misery visited upon one another,
when it is only you and I and them over there
waving our arms, wagging our tongues. So many
generals & strategists working the numbers,
the satellite photographs, the borders of great corporations
large as countries, measuring bottom lines
down to a teaspoon of blood & dimes. But

measurement is in everyone's eyes,
a glass half empty or full, and as the last bell tolls
a moment of quiet happiness comes,
and I am overwhelmed, wonder how many moments
there will be, when do they come, why do they go,
what if just now this almost intolerable *yes* to life lingered,
simultaneous, not just in me, but for one long breath,
an axis of sanity tilting the world just so—a president
pausing in oval office, eye caught by some tenderness
out the window; and a father in Kansas, or Illinois,
pausing over garden hoe, thankful for sons past the age
of recruiting. And a woman in Iran, forgiving the tyranny
of arrogant countries, standing near the wild terrain at dusk
praising the silence. And a naval officer tunneling beneath
acres of water, suddenly unable to conceive of pushing
the button, no matter the order that comes. And the young
brides of countless soldiers, caring only vaguely for the great
themes of war, praying that the brown, the blue, the hazel
beauty of husband's eyes will return; and the children, always
the children, suddenly remembered, legion upon legion—
before they grow, forgetful,

grumbling into small corners of the globe,
stuck in corner cubes of high-rises, dark corners of desert mosques,
humming hallways of missile silos where small dreams,
once broken, become large, ominous,
waking in the middle of night.

Of Shoes & Missiles

Today, an Egyptian diplomat was attacked,
Palestinians throwing shoes as he entered a mosque to pray.
I thought *this is progress*. So much of the world remains
uncertain—a wound scabbed, picked at, never left alone.
It is the new millennium, but today the paper announces
Russia has deployed a fresh batch of top-of-the-line nuclear missiles—
and I fear it is because of my own country's arrogance.
Bullies eyeing each other in the alley, touting the size
of cocks, fists.

I remember a professor describing how an *eye for an eye*
was once revolutionary, curbing brutality's extravagance:
not taking an arm too, a brother, a village. Now we risk
whole continents, a single atmosphere—still, the generals
plot acceptable levels of carnage, how a few relish surviving,
being right.

Would that it were a matter of prayers, of thrown shoes—
that when it comes to anger, we'd know the relevance of size,
how a planet feels in the palm of your hand,
how easy it is to stumble, let go.

Peace March

Scottish bagpipes were the reason,
the belly dancers rhythmical pulse,
or maybe it was the flags:
American, United Nations, Earth,
Bahai youth handing out heart stickers
emblazoned with *there is no room here for hatred.*

It could have been
the Spanish dancers, children in blue, red, white dresses
clicking hard-toed heels to music that says
every country is mine, with no lines to cross
but the curve of horizon glinting dark then light,
the satellite eye true—blue & brown, water & ground
all that lies beneath.

Armies are blind, but not the ones who point them,
   this is the reason
children were marching, this is the reason
Arab congregation, Jewish temple, Christian lesbians,
politicians for peace turned out
for this day

the art of survival, a new revival,
each shoe looking for another
to walk in

before the other shoe drops.

Silhouettes

The dark gray green browns of the massive oak two houses down
are part of one color, blending with infinite shades of cloud
silhouetted behind. Sitting in the cupola window, I hear
innumerable stories murmur & babble together—
all part of one weather, one day—a stream
becoming a river, a sea, a storm. Inside

this old house, built in 1912, one family after another
slept and woke in the same air I move in now, silhouettes
too dim to be seen—as Kelsey ponders in the room
that was an attic, as Gabriel slides belly-first down stairs
that materialized only later, as Linda sits by the window
that was a porch, as I write poems that will one day be
silhouettes too, indelibly imprinted in the ethers, settling
beneath the floorboards of the old house, nestled next
to the concrete foundation, becoming a small part
of its history, its tone, what it has learned to love.
Far away

in the caves of Afghanistan, tunneled deep beneath
frozen mountains rising like prayers from the barren plains,
soldiers kneel, bowing straight as a bullet for Mecca,
reciting hypnotic verse ancient as desire, as revenge
against those who would own you, one devil begetting
another till we are all the same, living in a pool of malice;
but a rifle like a pen can strike far, words sprung
as cluster bombs hoping to touch who we can with our fury,
our pain—and so each of us as a soldier waits beneath
our mountain while this war that is not a war goes on,
the pall of planes and rhetoric flashing like silhouettes
across late night TV. In the end,

Einstein was only partially right, sitting idly
in his Swiss patent office, ruminating on the origins of it all,
the relativity of time, the stunning equation that matter
was only a kind of light—insights a failed high school
education brings. But what he could not yet see
was the scintillating melody of *Superstring* theory:
that smaller than atom, than proton, neutron, electron,
smaller than quark or muon, was a field of infinitesimally
small vibrating strings, moving whichever way the bemused
scientists wished. And I wonder, do we play
upon these strings as a viola our deepest wishes,
silhouetting intimate chords of pain & pleasure—
the chaos you dream of, the world at its core resonating
your own strange music, the cacophony of sound
emanating in each new day a symphony we don't
yet know how to be. In the mean time,

the dark gray green browns of the massive oak two houses down
are all part of one color, one weather, one life—blending
with infinite shades of cloud moving over the globe
as a story, each story a silhouette of what may yet come,
murmuring & babbling as a river, a storm, a sea—
and here we are, immersed in the tide of this life
heaving from shore to shore.

All Hallows Eve

The oak log burns black and orange in the fireplace—
the colors of this night. A season of ghouls & ghosts,
neighborhood lawns strewn with tombstones,
the cackling laughter of garish pumpkin faces,
dark robed warlocks with red eyes drifting
from door to door, the laughter of children
dressed in the macabre, the fanciful,
some beautiful, some silly. It is

a night we are twisted inside out—shadows
emerge gremlin-like, celebration of all that is dark inside,
the masks we bear worn now for all to see—leering eyes,
painted cheekbones, crimson horns as much of what we are
as the simpler, sober faces worn everyday. I poke the fire,
answer the door again, offer the large black cauldron of candy
to yet another circle of beaming spirits, heroes, villains—
honor the truth gleaming in each eye. Later,

while parents drink red wine round the dining room table,
our children spread their booty on the floor—count, order,
trade candy as pirates, as manic traders on the stock exchange.
Meanwhile, around the globe: costumed soldiers prepare
for war, long-toothed vampires pretend the human, dress
as black-suited business men, sink the pointed edge of fang
into desert, brown skin, red heart—the mask of a president
leering across the sea at his fetish of oil. I, too,

am demon and hero. There are many ways to fail, many ways
to change a world. Not easy to tell which we do, what part
we play. Beneath this shiver of skin, this costume separating
you from me, we dance as a great being wearing each as a mask.
Down these streets, across the wide continents—glowing black
here, orange there—billions of eyes peer out, strain to see who
is there, beneath it all—the mystery of what we are,
this All Hallows Eve.

Napa Valley, Before the End

In Calistoga, local coffee roastery on the edge of town—
plumes of white steam from surrounding hot springs elevate
into cloud, become them. From this old wooden bench,
it looks like smoke, like war. I fall in love with the green of hill,
the grapes hanging from vine, not yet pressed into the business
of spirits. Like me, if lucky, some will grow old, happy, wrinkled—
most find their way to the bottom of a barrel, ferment for years,
become something new. The morning paper next to me

can't bear to be opened, afraid of what we've become, the sadness
of a messenger trumpeting victory as everything falls apart. I listen
to the three men lounging young and tormented at adjacent table,
mulling the night before, the intricacies of hangover, a beer to get
out of bed, caffeine and cigarettes to survive. They ruminate
on the need for money, how to make ends meet before the world ends
in white plume of smoke, in overcast sky—and I wonder,
this morning, is it that far off: the clouds full of faces, disappearing.

Ozone's Koan

When cars began to roam American streets, cities became cleaner. The stench of horse manure and urine, gone. Yesterday's miracle now fills the sky with choking grey. And death, kept at yapping bay with medicine's marvels, waits patient: there are too many of us to solve the puzzle. Every move is toward checkmate, every solution a new rubric that threatens. So the Zen masters knew: the unsolvable koan is to be lived—the broad sweep of kings and pawns how the game goes on. An invisible hole in the sky opens, the sun's radiance burning. The world is a terrible beauty, the heart a desperate riddle, breaking us, breaking us open.

Fundamentals

My life is cocooned in its own pace,
while the world moves at unfathomable speeds.
Mountains grow, barely noticing these few breaths
faint as moth wings—while universes explode
& collapse in the backyard. Tiny gnats live & die
while I take out the garbage, tread through autumn grass.
Old stone sits next to me, cannot see what I am.
The sudden storm believes I will live forever,
standing in the rain, bellowing. In this way,

all things are possible—gophers underfoot
build their tunnels heedless to fence or boundary,
forest shrinking in a China nameless to koala
nibbling bamboo, and those Russian hills
glowing faint with the soft light of plutonium,
half-life of eons barely begun. We all go on
forever—the particles of one thing
much like another, the smaller you get,
the more alike in essence. If this were

enough, I'd stop complaining right now.
But the moon, unappreciated by solar ray,
saves its beauty for me alone this night—

an eye for seeing, this human savoring,
this wagging tongue for telling.

Higher Than Birds

Start with a premise, that the sun
despairing at last of its own heat, will nova
into radiant dust. That we who are here now
vaguely care about such inevitability. That it is enough
trouble keeping water clean, air full of holes so large
Antarctica could fall through, be lost. Even the premise of ozone
begs the question: are we too smart for our own survival?
To see the invisible and not know awe, only the pang
of hairspray, of diesel fume: this is not a good sign.

Start with the premise that nine of the world's ten most
polluted cities lie in China, that one in every four humans
is Chinese, that they are cold, can now afford coal, its pall
of smoke. Start with the premise that America's footprint
is size twenty-five, the percent of timber, minerals, wetlands
we consume, the pollutants we pour in, the earth warming,
seas rising. Start with the premise that, together, we may
simply eat, spawn, spew the world into oblivion. Start

with the premise that an alcoholic must hit bottom, know
the gutter, before sanity sets in. Start with the premise of fear.

Once in a plane, flying low over the heartland, I could see
the Mississippi swollen as a snake, twisting as if to shed
old skin, convulse into something new. The land below
looked tired, brown—but the clouds were ethereal,
a kind of heaven where nothing was dirty, used up. A child
in the row behind me, looking out the window at the soft light,
chimed *Momma, we're higher than the birds!* It is only here,
　　　　the world pristine
in cirrus and cumulous, that innocence remains. Below, the rage
of patient earth: glacial, molten, the premise that we will be
　　　　outlasted
from sea to shining sea.

Manifest Destiny

Black ants scramble from rotten hole inside cedar round as the orange maul splits it in two. The swirl of hard wood knotted from where a branch once grew deterred many an axe before, protecting the soft decay beneath where ants had found a home. Now, a bigger tool has made their refuge useful—hence, dangerous.

How far must I go to become useless, to be of so little concern that the great machines of progress pass me by?

The Weather Gods

A relentless and lethal blanket of heat
settled on the southwest, canceling plane flights,
stoking wildfires, leaving twenty dead,
the homeless huddled in slivers of shade.
Miles north, before reading the headlines,
I blessed this unusually warm weather—
how the fickle gods had finally turned
their face towards me.

This Remembering

On the Klamath River near the Oregon border,
heading south out of Happy Camp, we river-raft down a gorge
ribbed with granite, oak & pine. Turtle River guides Isaac, Meadow,
Ken (who has been on the river 25 years) take our three rafts
& two kayaks through the Dragon's Tooth rapids
to our camping spot on the sand, prepare a grand meal,
then gather round the hot coals as humans have done for eons.
Ken has brought a Martin guitar, bagged and insulated
against the river, and so every night several of us take turns
playing Taylor, Young, Dylan, or the simple sounds of string
mixing with streaming water and the moods of night. Isaac
starts reciting poems from memory, all my favorites from Bly's
Rag & Bone Shop collection: Stafford, lots of Rumi, Mary Oliver,
Machado *as though golden bees were making honey from my old failures*—
the white-orange coals, the river, the moon hidden behind the cliff,
graciously, so that innumerable luminous stars can be seen. And bats
almost invisible in the luxurious dark of sand, sedge & willow
swoop silent over our camp, look to see who it is that sits by the river
swooning so—humans drunk with remembering

how to live simply with the earth—and we, preparing to return
more as lovers than petulant kings.

Heaven On Earth

We were gathered in the sand at the end of our trip
rafting along the river. I turned to Myra,
mother of a young river guide, asked where she lived.
Mount Shasta was the reply, telling her story
of the seventies when hippies began to move there,
drawn by the mountains magnetic tug,
finding their way among the rednecks & ranchers,
decorating their own pick-up trucks with tie-die rainbow-colors
where the gun racks used to be. I asked Myra what she did now
when not on the river. *Teach*, she said—and I wondered
what grade, thinking of my own children, but learned
she was a different kind of teacher, elucidating the ways
of Egyptian priestess in ancient *Mystery Schools*:
the skills of intuition, clairvoyance, clairaudience.
When Isaac, the lead guide, drew us together asking
what our experience on the river was, Myra spoke,
her eyes shining black as scarab beetles:
it is this, right here, these moments—this heaven on earth.
It was then I believed: the way the river shapes you,
bends you into a true life.

What We Might Become

Floating past cliffs of Alder, Madrone, into the shaded inlet
blanketed with green Indian Rhubarb like great elephant ears
along the bank. We leave our rafts, trek the mile upstream,
weaving our way through fallen scrabble of stone,
into scooped basins of water so cold your breath escapes
from lung, hovers just overhead. Finally, there it is,
tucked back behind a cavernous pool, tumbling down the towering cliffs
encircling us: Hiname Falls. Our young guide, Isaac, tells us
it was the flood of '65 that tore immense timbers from the mountain,
rushed them down the river to lodge in a cacophony of mangled wood
lodged against granite at the lip of the high falls. We watch him
swim across to the other side, pull himself up and climb along
hand and foot-holds till he disappears behind the torrent of water—
then emerges on the other side to stand in shade, wringing
his long length of black hair dry, arching like a being not quite wild,
but animal nonetheless, a part lost in those of us watching, huddled,
on the opposing rock-face. Something in me stirs, growls,
haunches springing into the electric cold, swimming across
to grope my way up till I stand on the mossy rock
next to the calamity of thunderous water. There is

a secret way *through* the falls, Isaac says, clamping hand and foot
tight to the rock-wall while letting the rumble of river tumble
over head and shoulder. But I am not strong enough, yet,
respect too much the watery beast plunging powerfully
inches from my face into the depth below—take the measure
of foolishness & bravery, twin souls capable of great feats,
great damage. Still, I launch myself off the rock-wall
just to the side of the falls, find myself in the numbing cold
underwater, thrust my limbs upward toward air. Surfacing,
my feet find a raised sand-bar and I stand chest-high in water
staring up at power so naked I worship unabashed.
There is a kind of prayer uttered in such moments,
so pure you barely care what form your life takes:

this defiant boundary carefully defended each waking day;
or what you might become, tumbling into the greater falls,
pummeled into a shape more liquid, flowing over stone
& jag as though nothing could ever bruise you again.

A Crack Between Two Worlds

A Crack Between Two Worlds

I remember Paul, his diagnosis: schizophrenia—and who could argue.
Sitting across from me on the edge of his chair, eyes like Jupiter moons,
alive with the secret he kept but shared with me now: that the solar system
was his, as far as Saturn's rings, maybe even beyond. Then there was me:
world shrunken to my perimeter of body, the narrow passage of mind,
the dull glare of reality. When it comes to this machine of brain,

the *true* or *false* litmus of belief, there is only one test here: sanity,
or its opposite. What poet could pass such exam without cheating,
what artist answer with any confidence? There is a crack in the world,
full of names—calling us to peer in, pull out our own secret
from the bowels of earth. A radio dial

spans a wide band of frequency, but even this is too narrow a gauge.
Beyond what we can hear, see, lies the farther spectrum
of infrared light, rays of gamma, pitch of sound so high as to drive
a dog crazy—while we look about blankly, hear nothing. It is good
to be careful. The closer you listen, you risk losing—an ear, a career,
a life. But what is horizontal in us begs the vertical, to meet here
in the body as a cross, to spread arms and legs wide saying
touch the holes in my hands, the holes in my feet,
feel the wound in my side. Even our gods

are over the edge. So this is what we face: everyday,
to be a ladder into the crevice, to pull ourselves out again,
whichever side we stand upon, to be a bridge for the other,
a thread for the wounds between.

The Middle World Where We Live

At the conference, she sat on stage telling her story: about the onset of mania so sweet God could be felt, intimate—the world finally making sense. How she shed her clothes on the shore, her jewelry in the sea— swimming naked towards a sense of arrival, some greater thing awaiting her in the waves beyond. And when the police helicopters circled,

urging her back to shore, how she went, dutifully, more naked than before—gold & diamonds lost under wave. The days in the psych- ward, the thick-tongued medication rooting her in body & bone. And then, walking out again into the soberness of never arriving—the clarity of doubt, the fickle dance of meaning—the world again a mix of heaven, and its absence.

The Spell

In Peete's Coffee, a young man sits by the window on a wooden stool, grimacing under weather-darkened skin. Fidgeting irritably when another man sits near to share the light, he bolts to a far empty table, face tense, reddening. A woman with a baby and blonde toddler carry hot chocolate and pastries toward the three empty seats at his table, asks if they are free. He says *yes*, face softening as the little girl chats amiably, looks him in the eye, smiles. For a moment, it is as though an immense beast lifts from his body, withdrawing talons, allowing the skin around his eyes to soften, smooth. The little girl's voice a spell, taming his demons till they purr like sated kittens curled in the corridors of his skull.

The Cage

Psychology has no self-help manual for its own affliction.
— James Hillman

Sitting amid the endless piles of notes on his desk,
the pages of explanation filling volumes on his shelves,
the psychologist feels impotent. Not his penis,
which sits flaccid against the careful boundary of his zipper,
blindly nosing toward each life that sits before him
as a dog sniffing for leftover food, dead animals,
the urine that marks the territory of other lives.
This impotence is deadlier: the maze of diagnostic reduction
deflating what was human, till it is limp. The linking of malaise
to childhood, to the womb, to anywhere but here, this moment:
the bleary-eyed artist that threatens, each hour, to waken,
to paint a new life from innumerable failures. But

unrelentingly they come, *forgive me father for I have sinned,*
there is something wrong, I can tell, you must fix it,
eradicate each defense mechanism, those little roaches,
keeping me dirty, making their little nests behind every wall,
every locked door, there must be an explanation, a medication,
fast-acting, time-released, a behavioral intervention to scold me,
a strategic theory to explain me, an ontological cure, an eraser
to return me past every psychological crime to the purity
of the reason, the answer I am. He blinks,

lifts the pen lying idly on the straight lines crossing
the white page as a cage, writes *grandiosity, mania*—
this false messiah, hoping to change what we are:
the melancholy of symphonies, the anxious glory of frescoes,
the drowning whirlpool of unbearable words only the wounded
may speak—and this we would bind, the labeling of symptoms
a mantra, a totem to ward away the evil eye, the one that defies

each attempt to cure this warped heart, a daemon that knows
nothing of disease, of category, of cure—only beauty,
every perverse form it takes. Broken, he lifts the leaking pen
from the page, leaves its stain. The door opens, in walks

the next patient, shuffling towards the therapy chair
as a man on death row, one who believes in electricity,
how its voltage can change you, release you from the human,
its schizophrenic demands. Throwing his broken pen away,
the psychologist rises from the desk, shows his patient the door,
follows down the stair to the undiagnosed street—*sees*
the street-corner preacher, the petulant young thief,
the bruised prostitute, the poet winking as if to say
ain't it something, man—this life without cure,
without the need to make it better
before the beauty can be seen.

Prophecy

Browsing amid rows of calendars—images of Tibetan buddhas, Frida's
deer with a crown of thorns—a white-bearded street musician enters
the store calling out for pictures of the Virgin Mary, railing against *the
Machine*, in anguish that we don't open our eyes more and *See!* He turns,
glares at my silver whiskers, bellows *those with white beards are like gods
rising from the depths to testify truth*—then walks out of the store continuing
his tirade. For only a moment, I am afraid he might be wrong about us.

What Is It Worth

On the tide-pools next to surging waves
stands a man in red-hooded sweatshirt, shorts, boots:
dancing. Kicking his legs out, he pounds, hops, skips—
I wonder what music he hears, and why I am not listening.

Above on the cliff, a woman sits holding a faded orange umbrella
over her head, dawdling her legs beneath a bench.
It is not raining, though she seems happy enough to wait.
Dressed in purple jacket, flowered pants, pink high-top shoes,
I think she is from the same country as the dancing man below—
where you go when, long past caring, the world is worth
waiting for, dancing to.

The Small Body Of the Human

The plane was delayed, so rather than drive to pick up loved ones,
I wake slow—the morning hours extravagantly spent
tumbling in & out of sleep, of sexual reverie—
such simple delights that the gods, at creation,
offered as balms for the terrible loneliness of the human.
Then outside, down the wide boulevard to the sea,
twenty-eight pelicans glide gracefully by, just over the cliffs,
barely moving a wing, carried by wind, meandering. There
is a kind of loneliness that is like sex, or sleep, when the world
is made only for you, when it unfolds symbiotic as a dream,
everything you meet a symbol of your heart, your fear,
your hidden longing. And so the two Harley-Davidson bikers
standing next to their chromed choppers, black helmeted heads
staring out to sea, are beautiful in a way that can't be named.
And the red brick lighthouse, so unnecessary in all this calm & light,
waits patiently to be essential, to save someone's life.
And the green hippie-bus emblazoned with slogans that, if followed,
would yield a life anyone might die for. I could almost jump
on-board, be driven from town to town, a hobo-god heir
to a vast land where nothing is owned and you're the richer
for it. But isn't this the case already? Nothing can be held
for long, though every moment is willing to surrender—
each motorcycle, wing, brick a way of loving the world.
  But I have my small life, carried about stingily
as so much change in pocket—too little even for a quarter
in the open violin case of the old man playing along the road.
This is when the lighthouse is supposed to save me, or lure
toward the jagged boulders the inadequate boat that is my life,
teach me to swim in the wild sea. If everyday were like this,
I couldn't bear the beauty—so wander home at last, fall
into sleep and dream the dream of waking, again, lonely,
   in the small body of the human.

Blue In the Face

You conceive a few molecules, the *self*
compressed as sperm penetrating a wall, but it is more than this,
you have already been born, it is the second one, riskier
than the first, more fundamental, the beginning of the you inside,
nurtured along as a pale flame in the cold that everything else
will depend upon—it grows, consuming fiber, teeth, neurons,
till the whole body, the forests of hair, the oceans of blood
are bulging with the possibility of birthing yourself anew,
but you never do—

then you read the newspaper, knowing what it is to die
before you emerge, and the story is not about you but of course
        it is—
she had hidden herself for nine months
beneath black sweaters, trusting the light to reflect a different truth,
even the boy she danced with in the dark knew nothing,
was not the father, barely beyond his own mother's womb,
not enough to notice his young date's mound, maybe she
was just gaining weight, but man ,she looked good anyway,
promised her everything, anything for just one
        pop—
        that was why
when the flood began to flow through the breach in her legs
down into her spiked shoe, she ran towards the alley alone
with her secret life, spilled it out, did not wait for a cry,
wrapped the phosphorescent blue skin of her baby
in one story after another of yesterday's newsprint,
burying her new life deep in the bottom of the trash bin
before her date would notice because he was the only hope—
        it is difficult to explain
how we run from ourselves, there are many reasons not to become
what it is we want—but the oceans of blood are rushing,
the forests of hair are afire, every neuron gnashing because

it is more than teeth, more than skin, more than hope for a better life,
    it is this—
you wake blue wrapped in other people's stories,
it is only this scream, this first in-then-out of air—then you have it,
then you know, then you begin.

Sizing Up the World

There's nothing here of interest to me
said the fat boy with glasses, head buried in yet another book,
when asked why he didn't pay more attention
to what was going on. I couldn't blame him,
straddled as I was between worlds—the interior mind
endless as a multiverse, the exterior world boring as a parking lot,
but stubbornly real. Now the other boys could make a parking lot
infinitely interesting, with their pickup trucks and speed demon cars
parked & purring while the girls with short skirts and tan legs sidled up,
fawning. But beyond this, it was just bowling alleys & garbage-can alleys
where boys grew to be men, balls in the gutter, throwing their lives away.
It's tough when you reach your pinnacle at eighteen, slide down
the backside as though there was really someplace to go,
but there's not—prom king & queen surveying the small town
they'd inherit, eyes fading into the dusky blur of a world too small
for dream. Except for the nerd with glasses, slipping down
backside of the skull, imagination rollicking around the cranium
with telescope & microscope, universes rolling off the page
as a careening big-bang. He was a prophet of sorts,
sacred books of science fiction & fantasy opening as portals
the dark side of moon, the rage of demon-dragons, the light
that would not be put out—even as the football jocks
would pass us in the hallway, jostle & insult a daily gauntlet,
as though the darkness had taken sneering shape
in high school corridor and locker room hell. It was then
I decided that heroism was no fantasy, that this planet
was stranger than most, that I would need to keep my wits
about me, would need to become a wizard of sorts to survive
on this rickety bridge between worlds—that everything
going on merited my full attention—the world a bloated
      story,
and I, bespectacled devourer of universes,
holding the key to how mine
would turn out.

Universal Studios

The CityWalk next to the Sheraton hotel
throbs with magnetic energy, full-throttle entertainment
skittering out elaborate cartoonish restaurant & shop facades,
through the milling hordes, the enormous outdoor movie screen
lit up with music videos barreling bass & drum & guitar tracks
straight through my spinal cord and out heels, shoulders—
and I feel it, this rakish sales job, begin to shimmy my walk a bit,
a little jive in my step, can't seem to help it
as I saunter past the Mexican café adorned with original paintings
hung on fabulously hued walls, stare at one in the courtyard,
this black & grey portrait of a fallen angel, backside angle
with the eye peeking over one huge wing, the glance intoxicated,
as though saying *it's been worth every penny*. What is this

penchant for being filled, for taking it all in—am I glutton
or tantric monk, shuttling along the studio tour face-to-face
with *Jaws'* insatiable shark, *King Kong's* raging face & fists,
diving underground into subway movie-set where the big-quake hits,
the cement pillars crumble, and the waters come flooding in
(again & again). I let myself go,

fall into each story, each block another world: Rome here,
old New York there, frontier towns filled with so many characters
you want to become them all (is this what God felt?), awash
in heroism & intrigue & near escapes—drama so necessary
to keeping desire alive, because the play's the thing. Who
wants to be the prude—words like *sin, maya*—when every excess
is someone's joy? Like the two Buddhist nuns standing in line
several aisles ahead, eyes alive with enlightened mischief,
laughing so hard at each new sight & sound
that I suddenly know:

my life's worth every cent paid.

Nebuchadnezzar's Stone

In the British Museum, a mahogany room
of rare books, antiquities, archaeological treasures.
On one shelf, low to the floor, a stone fragment
from Babylon filled with hieroglyphs from millennia ago.
Beyond wildest dream, a voice survives the indignity:
ravages of dust, memory, the burden of meaning.
 The names, they change, but listen:
everyone who has lived is breathing in your skin still:
desire, calling for witness.

At San Marcos Square

The old Muslim,
black coat, faded burgundy hat,
face so dark & wrinkled I could not begin to understand.
Sometimes standing, head bowed, cup held out for coin.
Or kneeling, face pressed to the ground in the heat of day:
I could feel wealth burning in my palm, a handful of *euros*
that mean so little, so much. And still,
poverty that neither empire nor spirit can fill.

Outside the Cathedral

"...the birds neither toil nor weep."

My son & daughter sit cross-legged, arms raised
as pigeons come to feed from the seed
scattered on legs, outstretched arms, head. Nearby,
towering spires, four bronze horses, centuries of Venetian art:
but this, their happiest moment. I see the young beggar
under the arch: legs too short, broken forward at the knee,
watching from the shade. Hundreds of bags,
a single coin each, his cup empty.

Surrender

This hill town of Montalcino was fought over
by Siena and Florence, so many kings, popes.
A deep pacifist, I nonetheless feel what they must
have: standing, looking over the valley below—
rolling fields of grape & wheat, sun & cloud tirelessly
seductive: there are things you never want to lose,
will fight to keep, even if it means the death of you.

Fear, Skin, Power

On the walls of my room at the villa,
framed pictures of Victorian women neck to foot
in elaborate gowns. In my book, I read that Qatar
—oil-rich, traditional Arab—allows women to vote,
run for office, drive, though covered head to toe
save for eye slits. I think of this on the beach in Italy—
amid thongs, bare breasts—what it is we hide,
allow, and why. Whether the danger
is in what we uncover, or cover.

The Lost Goddess

As a Protestant child, I never understood
the presence of Mary in the Catholic Church,
how she became the Mother of God—but now,
so obvious, standing before her in the Siena cathedral
encircled by the stone faces of popes, this world
of men butchering, indulging, ruling as though
the penis were a cross, a weapon, a war—
how she holds her son, soothing his male body,
how he surrenders.

Food For Thought

He stood at the corner of the busy intersection—black beard, raven eyes, bright red shirt—a cardboard sign scrawled with the words *traveling, stranded, hungry*. In the eyes of we commuters, a different kind of hunger for what it was possessed him—daemon of an itinerant god, who wanders, feeds on lost grief, prays we remember why we are here.

Abandoned Clay

Taking Gabriel to his new school, he grabs my hand, shows me around, kisses my neck. At last embrace, I look up, catch the eye of an older kid watching, who looks quickly away. But I see him—the way soft clay hardens when left alone.

Island Of the Sharers

When Magellan dropped anchor in the bay, the Chamorros paddled out
to greet him in swift *proas*—amazed they were not alone in the world.
Having no concept of property, they shared coconut & fish with starving
sailors, in return taking marvelous iron tools & brass mirrors without
asking. For this, after burning forty houses and killing seven men, the
captain christened this land Islas de los Ladrones—Island of Thieves.

Still, the Chamorros grieved when the marvelous strangers
left, unaware they would never again be alone.

The Endless Quest

In Magellan's time, spice ruled the world rather than oil.

Whole countries decimated for the right to trade, control.
Then, as now, no end in sight: the world a beast,
insatiable, craving.

Watch us chase black gold beneath earth—
and soon, the golden dark of space: a last mirage.

Witnessing

Not rich enough to really care about money, but enough to take   for granted this vacation with my daughter. On our tiny kitchen table: a red-green apple, an orange, a perfect banana. Outside, hot springs to ease the body's ache, but one: so much of this world still hungry, still cruel.

Another Ordinary Day

Flying into New York, I am surprised by spontaneous applause erupting from everywhere in the plane as we land. An uneventful trip, though I too scanned the skyline for missing towers, dangers. How we stand and clap over such gorgeous, ordinary feats as another day.

A Cure For What Is Human

Late at night, turning the television on, I watch congressional hearings about soldiers returning from war, the mysterious illnesses, the government uncaring. Then testimony from physicians about the need for animal testing—torturing mice with chemicals of war to find a cure for humans. With this kind of thinking, will we ever find a cure for what ails us?

Am I Awake Or Asleep?

John Lennon on a bumper sticker: *I may be a dreamer, but I'm not the only one*—such nostalgic sentiment. Then, two cars later, an identical message—and suddenly, in my own heart, I know I am not alone in this dream.

Dante's Spoons

A massive sculpture fountain sits just down from the Capitol
outside the Sacramento Convention Center.
Morphing from granite contours are many faces:
Sumerian, Japanese, European—as though humanity
was a many-faced creature eschewing from the same body,
not quite animal, not quite spirit—confused as to origin,
destination, but magnificent. Along the base, a question
is carved on each of the four stone sides:
> *Where Are We Going...*
> *What Have We Thought...*
> *How Are We Loving...*
> *What Have We Wrought?*
And I think that government is essentially
a spiritual nurturing gone astray, how the circle
of citizens quibble over tax codes & loopholes
rather than hunger, health—how the heart
beats in such isolated synchrony when the song
of *me & mine* is the only tune playing, the great
questions etched silent, abandoned to stone,
forgotten. Entering the building adjacent,

I take an elevator to the twelfth floor
where we sit in black leather swivel chairs,
tan carpet & polished wood tables stretching across
the windowed room. Seasoned committee members
ponder legislative bills, policies, statistics:
every *yea* or *nay* the small butterfly wings
that turn to hurricane or balm the welfare
of those living outside this white citadel.
I remember Dante's story,

the simple difference between heaven & hell.
In two rooms, the same large soup bowls,
the same impossibly long-necked spoons—
but in hell, the endless failure of feeding alone;
and in heaven, the ease of dipping each long spoon,
lifting it to your neighbor's lips, the joy
of being fed in return.

The Secret Dreams Of Committees

To cooperate.
To collude in possibilities, to confederate,
be in league with, unite one's efforts,
keep together, pull together, hang together, hold together, band
together,
lay heads together,
act in concert,
join forces,
understand one another,
hunt in couples,
play ball.

To side with, go along with,
make common cause,
mix oneself up with,
take part in, cast one's lot with,
rally around, follow and lead,
throw in with,
line up with,
be in the same boat with.

Be a party to, lend oneself to, participate,
have a hand in, have a finger in the pie,
sit in, chip in,
play the game of,
espouse a cause or quarrel

partake, be in cahoots,
as one being,
together, unanimously,
shoulder to shoulder,
side by side,
hand in hand,
in common,
share and share alike

synchronize
harmonize
organize
dream.

HEARTHEARTHEARTHEARTHEARTHEART

Not far from the Capitol in Sacramento, a civic artist chiseled this scripture in concrete. While lobbyists down the street scheme who can hoard the most, I sit on the sidewalk and open my *heart* to *hear the earth*, this *art* my *hearth*, open my *ear* to *hear* this *art heart*, this *earth art*, my own *heart*.

The Shining Path

Route 92 branches off from the coast highway,
begins to weave sinuous down a corridor of Eucalyptus.
On my way to hear a Federal official speak, I veer
onto this scenic road past green fields with small white goats,
Obestor Winery grapes, blanketed valley of flowers—
hear the bleating, almost taste the wine, scattered fragrance
seeping into the car's ventilation—become intoxicated.
Think *every meeting should begin this way*, the scent of petals
luring the heart into decisions it should have made all along.

Caught behind a yellow Caterpillar backhoe,
I slow to a happy crawl—another excuse to meditate.
Notice sun illuminating the beet & artichoke sign
posted on the old telephone pole, suddenly question
any sadness that lures the heart into resignation—
the world laid as a shining path waiting to be found-out.

Just then, the road opens—cars stream past
alluring curve of lake into sinuous curve of freeway
snaking as tangled legs, pulling me further into the city's body.
I follow sleek metallic creatures with names
like *jetta, altima, horizon*—seductive with direction—
wonder where it is we're headed with such blind
purpose. But inside the airport hotel I hear
a speaker lecture on the frequency of malaise,
the statistics of hope, how many are lost,
but that there is a way through.
　　And I believe what it means to be lost,
what the path is: this elusive, unmistakable snaking
toward the shining nucleus in each moment. How
there is really no place to go but *here*, how it is enough
to be the emptiness, the filling, the way the world wakes.

Atop the Parking Garage In Downtown Sacramento

Across the yellow span of bridge,
I enter the city as a pilgrim,
see the Capitol building white, hopeful, besieged
down the long lane—Embassy Suites on the right,
Macy's on the left, the office buildings
of every conceivable interest group lining the broad boulevard.
Claustrophobic on the one-way streets, the milling cars
crossing directions like the scarecrow in Oz,
I turn, relieved, into the Sheraton Regency parking garage,
take my ticket and drive to the very top, passing empty spaces
along the way. I love the lack of ceiling, the open air,
look out over the city, consider the old stone of cathedral
topped with four small crosses, the immense IMAX theater sign
in red & blue, the sleek windowed offices rising higher
as though Babel's towers were still ascending,
looking for comfort in the sky's perimeter—
for a firm, tangible hand to rest on the roof,
for a voice to say, just once:
Here, this is far enough to satisfy.

This Burning

In the dark ahead, it floats like an orange mirage,
eerie flame of light in the hills that surround Los Angeles
like taut, brown undulations—driving back from a conference
about youth, abused & neglected—how the world swims
in alternating waves of fierce light & infinitely dim
shades of despair. The plenary speaker with his grim tale
of childhood—the rapes, the abuse—how the system
saved his life, foster parents lifting him up
far enough to stand on his own DNA & the mysteries
of karmic spirit carrying his story to the New York Times,
his work to three presidential citations for excellence.
And the road winds higher through the night as the orange glow
grows brighter, flames lapping the black outline of swelling ground—
still too distant to be afraid—but the awe growing.
As with the next speaker, Azim—Persian born in Africa,
educated in England, financial consultant turned crusader
against the violence that took his son in the streets of San Diego,
college student delivering pizza unfazed by the bogus address
in the run-down neighborhood, the 14 year old gang-banger
waiting for him with the gun, told he'd become a man
by taking the other one down. And in the aftermath,
Azim finding the 14 year old boy's grandfather, saying
my son's death must come to mean something—
how they banded together bent on saving at least one more,
and another, then another. How his eyes burned
as I shook his hand, thanked him for his story,
told him it means everything—how I drove silently
in the night into the heaving hills afire, so close now,
not knowing if there would be a way through,
the black asphalt road leading inexorably
into the smoke-orange flame of the grapevine,
the only way out being through—and there it was,
the fire-break, the very road I was on, separating

Hades' heat on one side from the quiet untouched hills
on the other. In between, in this eerie safety
of windshield & engine & wheels, I see
there is but one way to travel this world,
and it is towards, not away,
from this burning.

Emancipation

In Cincinnati, the Underground Railroad museum is built on prime real estate by the river—a political act, to ease racial tensions still simmering these long years. At lunch, someone says *I can't see past the politics to appreciate this place*—but I say the escape from slavery is still going on. Hear the rustling of chains: our furtive hearts beating, longing.

Writers In the Schools

Leaving the border of Central Park, I wander into East Harlem with my poems to find Heritage School. Henry takes us upstairs, past security guards, brightly colored masks, into his ninth grade English class—where a roomful of beautiful brown and black faces peer cautiously back. After the reading, I listen to their poems—brutal angst, scathing beauty—and you can tell they almost know: the city cannot live without them.

Leaving a Mark

On the railways leaving London: miles of graffiti covering every inch of metal, brick, wood. Here, as everywhere, some coven of boys always restless, dying to be seen. It is no different in the cathedrals & museums, Trafalgar Square with its lions and columns:

something wants to leave a mark, to rise above. Would that a city could smelt its violence into tenderness: history made of more than winning, erecting, strutting. But in the meantime, even the pigeons leave their mark: decorating the spires of Parliament as they rest.

When Justice Goes Blind

The gardens of the Temple district,
once owned by the Knights Templar,
are now surrounded by law offices.
I stop at a circular fountain
with a sculpture of a small boy:
nude, except for a book
hovering as a fig leaf
inscribed with *Lawyers,*
I suppose, were children once...
Next door in the British high courts,
you can see them still
hiding naked behind piles of books
seeing who can pee the farthest.

Lions After Slumber

Poetry used to be worth the world, before resplendent
in literary silk, dead.

But in 1909, women of the Ladies Garment Union
pressed on against winter, scabs, prison
reciting *Mask of Anarchy* as they worked inside the
Triangle Shirtwaist Company in New York City:

Rise like lions after slumber, shake your chains
to earth...Ye are many, they are few!

When fire broke out in the rag bin, sweeping through
illegal floors with locked doors too high for the ladders
to reach, the New York *World* responded in lyric:

> *They jumped with their clothing ablaze...*
> *they leapt with their arms around each other,*
> *onto growing piles of the dead and dying.*

When it was over, one hundred thousand marched
down Broadway, because it mattered,
because the twenty seven thousand killed on the job
every year at the turn of this great century
made silent poems of their lives, because Joe Hill
was charged with murder as he sang, lyrics inciting
the downtrodden to throw off their chains
as gospel hymns the slaves before—

and because his poetry mattered, he was executed
by firing squad in Utah, calling man, woman and child,
black and white, immigrants all, to do something
tangible, now.

Which Langston Hughes did in the 30's,
wedding the poem to the world rather than the classroom,
calling to the people

> *Who made America,*
> *Whose sweat and blood, whose faith and pain...*
> *Must bring back our mighty dream again...America!*

Poetry must rise as a lion after slumber,
hunt game of import, roar with every stroke,
for we cannot matter to the world
if the world does not matter to us.

How the World Changes

The Exxon man smiled, extended his hand, saying
I'm just like you—the Viet Nam vet eyeing him warily,
then clasping the hand in return.

Everyone wants the same thing, he continued,
a fair shake, the chance to make your fortune in the world—
the farmworker wiping his brow, nodding—how could one disagree?

Loosening his tie, the Exxon man was just getting
worked up. *Can you believe before the Second World War
I paid ninety percent in taxes; is that fair*…the single mother
of three peering up from her night-school books after the long day,
dinner, homework, pajamas, nodding half asleep past midnight.
No, it didn't seem quite fair, but she wasn't sure.

*Our man in the White House was a real American,
put you and me in the same bracket; cut the welfare roles,
asked everyone to do their share*…the Exxon man speaking smooth
as a preacher now, spying another oil man seated in a wheelchair.
This oil man, too, wanted to do his share, even after the government
overruled the company doctor and the state supervisor testifying
he was no longer able to work. He didn't complain, limping back
into the black field.

The Exxon man smiled. It was the way it should be, everyone
chipping in, working hard, keeping the wheels turning.

Then the oil man died.

That same day, Federal officials gathered around the Exxon man,
comforting him. *Such bad luck,* they said, *but a public relations problem
you know. Not your fault, couldn't be helped.*

This is the way the world goes.

The next day, the Viet Nam vet, the farmworker, the single mother
stopped buying it, stopped buying everything, stopped watching TV,
stopped voting for the same tired politicians sponsored on both tickets
by every Exxon man and his cousin, stopped guzzling the hysterical
headlines of plane crashes and murders and the next dirty war,
the endless advertisements for everything you could possibly think
of and never need, stopped buying it all, just stopped—
started living rather than consuming.

This is the way the world changes.
The Exxon man shivered.
It seemed anti-American somehow, to not want things anymore—
the imperceptible crack in the edifice before it falls.

Poetry Should

Poetry should matter
like water

something to die for

necessary as air

bread
for the hungry
not

shelved, pristine
above the fray

each of us could speak
something

urgent from the bottom
of our lives

anything

with weight, levity
what is essential

is the speaking
as though lives depended
on it for

we do.

Notes

Endless appreciation to my fellow members of the **Emerald Street Writers**, who assisted with the development of many of these poems. Without them, my poetry might still be lumps of stone dreaming of emeralds: *Marcia Adams, Julia Alter, Len Anderson, Virgil Banks, Jenny D'Angelo, Guarionex Delgado, Kathleen Flowers, Carol Housner, Robin Lopez-Lysne, Joanna Martin, Phyllis Mayfield, Maggie Paul, Stuart Presley, Joan Safajek, Lisa Simon, Robin Straub, Phil Wagner.*

My work has been greatly influenced by a number of important Santa Cruz poets. In particular, I'd like to thank *Gary Young, Joseph Stroud, Maude Meehan, Robert Sward,* and *Ellen Bass* for their contributions to poetry, and the development of local poets.

In a similar vein, many thanks to **Poetry Santa Cruz** members for their tireless and devoted nurturing of the poetry landscape in the greater Monterey Bay: *Len Anderson, Dennis Morton, Julia Alter, Maggie Paul, Phil Wagner, Tilly Shaw, Marcia Adams.* Also, appreciation to *David Sullivan* for many years of nurturing Cabrillo College's *Porter Gulch Review*, and *Patrice Vecchione* for nurturing so many local poets.

Of course, without my community of family and friends, many of these poems would never have occurred. Thank-you for lending your children, thoughts, stories, shared experiences—and patience with showing up in some of my work.

In particular, love and appreciation to my wife *Linda* for her commitment to making poetry possible amid a full family life; to my children *Kelsey* and *Gabriel* for their laughter, love, and inspiration for much of my work; to my mother *Bonnie* and father *Del* for inspiration throughout this life, as well as my brothers *Steve, Scott,* and sister *Denise* for their creativity and commitment to the heart.

I'd like to acknowledge artist Trudy Kraft for her cover painting. Her work can be seen at http://www.trudykraft.com/

We Find Healing In Existing Reality

Plain View Press is a 32-year-old issue-based literary publishing house. We have published 175 titles and more than 300 writers from many countries. Our books result from artistic collaboration between writers, artists and editors. Over the years we have become a far-flung community of activists whose energies bring humanitarian enlightenment and hope to individuals and communities grappling with the major issues of our time — peace, justice, the environment, education and gender. This is a humane and highly creative group of people committed to art and social change. The poems, stories, essays, non-fiction explorations of major issues are significant evidence that despite the relentless violence of our time, there is hope and there is art to show the human face of it.

About the Author

Dane Cervine lives in Santa Cruz, California with his wife and two children, where he serves as Chief of Children's Mental Health for the county, as well as a consultant and trainer across the state.

Over 100 of Dane's poems have appeared in a wide variety of journals and magazines, ranging from small college and university presses, independent and on-line journals, newspaper and art museum publications — to Buddhist, Quaker, and Pagan magazines.

In April of 2005, Dane's poem "Saturdays" appeared in the *Hudson Review's New Writer's Edition,* for which he participated in a New York City debut reading. His poem "Engine" appeared in the November 2005 issue of *The SUN.* "The Jeweled Net of Indra" appeared in the September 2006 issue of *The SUN,* and was also chosen by Adrienne Rich as the winning poem for the National Writers Union 2005 competition. In January 2006, "Accordions & Shotguns" appeared in Purdue University's *Sycamore Review,* and was chosen as a finalist by award-winning poet Tony Hoagland for the Wabash Prize for Poetry.

The poet Maude Meehan describes his first book, *What A Father Dreams: Poems of Family, Love, & Aging:* "This collection of poems by Dane Cervine is a rich feast. An exploration of the joys and exigencies of family, commitment, parenting and deeply sensual love. We journey through an infinite variety of emotions and observations penned from an amazingly open heart. The lyric quality of this work delighted me."

In addition, a selection of chapbooks are available from the author at danecervine@cruzio.com or Dane's website: http://danecervine.typepad.com

Printed in the United States
74752LV00003B/211-309